Adobe®
GoLive™ 4.0

Classroom in a Book

Adobe

Contents

Getting Started

About Classroom in a Book 1

Prerequisites 1

Checking system requirements 2

Installing the program 2

Copying the Classroom in a Book files 3

Additional resources 3

Troubleshooting in Mac OS 4

Adobe certification 4

A Quick Tour of Adobe GoLive

Getting started 6

Creating a new site 7

Dragging and dropping to add files to a Web site 11

Designing a Web page 12

Previewing Web pages with Adobe GoLive 23

Creating a second Web page 24

Adding a predesigned Web page and animating it 30

Creating links 35

Managing sites 38

Previewing and testing files 40

Working with Text

Lesson 1 43

Getting started 44

Designing the Web page 45

Adding text 50

Formatting text 51

Creating lists 52

Adding a line break 54

Changing the color of text 55

Adding tables 56

Applying fonts 65

Editing text 67

Previewing the Web page in Adobe GoLive 69

	Exploring on your own	69
	Review questions	73
	Review answers	73

Laying Out Web Pages

Lesson 2	77
Getting started	78
Creating a new Web site	79
Adding files to the Web site	81
Creating a dynamic component	83
Designing the home page	93
Updating the design of the Appraisal page	101
Designing the Hottest Buy page	104
Editing a dynamic component	110
Previewing the Web pages in Adobe GoLive	111
Exploring on your own	112
Review questions	114
Review answers	114

Links

Lesson 3	119
About links	120
Getting started	121
Opening a site	122
Creating a link from a graphic	123
Creating anchors	129
Creating hypertext links	132
Creating an action	138
Using clickable image maps	140
Setting preferences for link warnings	149
Finding and fixing broken links	149
Previewing links	151
Review questions	152
Review answers	152

Working with Frames

Lesson 4	157
About frame sets	158
Getting started	159

Creating a frame set 161
Adding a frame set 161
Making changes to the frame set 163
Setting up the main content frame 165
Adding, moving, and deleting frames 167
Adding content to frames 169
Creating targeted links 171
Creating a link back to the home page 172
Linking the frame set to your home page 173
Review questions 174
Review answers 174

Animation   **Lesson 5** 177
Getting started 178
Creating rollovers 179
Working with floating boxes 182
Animating floating boxes 189
Animating multiple floating boxes 195
Actions 200
Review questions 208
Review answers 208

Forms   **Lesson 6** 211
Getting started 212
About forms 214
Creating a section of a form 215
Using the Custom tab of the Palette to store
and add objects 224
Adding an image that spans two columns 226
Adding radio buttons 228
Modifying a list box 231
Adding a clickable image 232
Adding a Reset button 234
Changing the main table's border and cell spacing 235
Creating a tabbing chain 235
Review questions 238
Review answers 238

Using Cascading Style Sheets

Lesson 7 241

Getting started 242

About style sheets 243

Exploring an internal style sheet 246

Creating a style sheet 257

Saving and linking a style sheet 259

Creating a class style 262

Duplicating a style 264

Changing the background color 265

Previewing the results in current browsers 267

Exploring on your own 269

Review questions 271

Review answers 271

Site Management

Lesson 8 275

About Adobe GoLive Web site management 276

Getting started 277

Importing an existing site into Adobe GoLive 279

Exploring the site in the site window 280

Exploring the expanded site window 283

Correcting errors 285

Managing folders 290

Adding new pages to your site 293

Using the Site Trash 295

Managing the Site view 296

Creating new pages in the Site view 305

Changing all hyperlinks and file references 308

Importing resources and removing unused ones 310

Exploring on your own 312

Review questions 314

Review answers 314

Index 315

Getting Started

Welcome to the Adobe® GoLive™ application—the essential tool for developing and managing Web sites. With Adobe GoLive, you can design and lay out Web pages with pixel precision, and you can manage and update your site resources with powerful site management tools.

You can also easily develop Web pages using the latest Web technology, such as cascading style sheets to format text, dynamic HTML to animate your pages, and ready to use JavaScript actions.

About Classroom in a Book

Adobe GoLive 4.0 Classroom in a Book® is part of the official training series developed by experts at Adobe Systems. The lessons are designed to help you learn at your own pace. If you're new to Adobe GoLive, you'll understand the fundamental concepts and features you'll need to master the program. If you've been using Adobe GoLive for a while, you'll find Classroom in a Book teaches many advanced features, including tips and techniques for using this latest version.

Although each lesson provides step-by-step instructions for creating a specific project, there's room for exploration and experimentation. You can follow the book from start to finish, or do only the lessons that correspond to your interests and needs. Each lesson concludes with a review section summarizing what you've covered.

Prerequisites

Before beginning to use *Adobe GoLive 4.0 Classroom in a Book*, you should have a working knowledge of your computer and its operating system. Make sure you know how to use the mouse and standard menus and commands and also how to open, save, and close files. If you need to review these techniques, see the printed or online documentation included with your system. You must also have the Adobe GoLive 4.0 application installed on your computer. Adobe GoLive 4.0 is not included in this package. To preview Web pages, you need a browser compatible with Netscape® Navigator® 4.0 or later, or one compatible with Internet Explorer® 4.0 or later.

Checking system requirements

Before you begin using *Adobe GoLive 4.0 Classroom in a Book*, make sure that your system is set up correctly. To use Adobe GoLive, you need the following hardware and software:

Windows

- 200 MHz Pentium® processor, or equivalent.
- Windows 98 or Windows NT® 4.0 (or later) with Service Pack 3.
- 24 MB RAM.
- 30 MB of hard disk space.
- Internet Explorer 4.0.

Mac OS

- An Apple® Power Macintosh® or 100% compatible computer.
- 24 MB (minimum) of free random-access memory (RAM). (32 MB is recommended.)
- 30 MB of hard disk space.
- Mac OS version 8.0 or later.

Playing and editing movies

If you're using Adobe GoLive on a Windows or Macintosh system, you can play and edit movies. To play movies, you need the following hardware and software:

- In Windows you need to have the appropriate sound and video boards installed in your computer, and Apple QuickTime® 3.0 or later software.
- On the Macintosh you need Apple QuickTime 3.0 or later.

QuickTime software is included as an installation option in the Adobe GoLive 4.0 installer.

Installing the program

You must purchase the Adobe GoLive software separately. For complete instructions on installing the software, see the install readme that comes on the application CD.

Copying the Classroom in a Book files

The Classroom in a Book CD includes folders containing all the electronic files for the lessons. Each lesson has its own folder, and you must copy the folders to your hard drive to do the lessons. To save room on your drive, you can install only the necessary folder for each lesson as you need it, and remove it when you're done.

To install the Classroom in a Book files for Windows:

1 Insert the Adobe GoLive Classroom in a Book CD into your CD-ROM drive.

2 Create a subdirectory/folder on your hard drive and name it **AG4_CIB**.

3 Do one of the following:

• Drag the Lessons folder from the CD into the AG4_CIB folder.

• Copy only the single lesson folder you need.

To install the Classroom in a Book folders for Mac OS:

1 Insert the Adobe GoLive Classroom in a Book CD into your CD-ROM drive.

2 Create a folder on your hard drive and name it **AG4_CIB**.

3 Do one of the following:

• Drag the Lessons folder from the CD into the AG4_CIB folder.

• Copy only the single lesson folder you need.

Additional resources

Adobe GoLive 4.0 Classroom in a Book is not meant to replace documentation provided with the program. Only the commands and options used in the lessons are explained in this book. For comprehensive information about program features, refer to these resources:

• The User Guide included with the Adobe GoLive software. This guide contains a complete description of all features.

• The Adobe Web site.

Troubleshooting in Mac OS

If you are using the Macintosh operating system, you need to be aware of two preference settings. The first concerns the shareware application Internet Config, which helps manage your Internet preferences. The second involves Apple's Navigation Services system enhancement.

Internet Config

There is a conflict between Adobe GoLive 4.0 and Internet Config. Adobe recommends that you never select the Use Internet Config option. By default the option is not selected, but there are three places you should check:

- Choose > Edit > Preferences > General > File Mapping > Use Internet Config.
- Choose > Edit > Preferences > Network > Internet Config Settings > Use Always.
- Choose > Edit > Preferences > Network > Up-/Download > Use Always.

The option Use Internet Config must be deselected in all three preference settings. If even one is active, you may encounter performance difficulties using Adobe GoLive 4.0.

Navigation Services

Navigation Services changes the appearance and behavior of the Open and Save dialog boxes. This feature is always available at the system level, and can be controlled on an individual application basis.

Due to conflicts between Navigation Services and Mac OS 8.5 and earlier, the lessons in this book do not use Navigation Services. By default Adobe GoLive 4.0 tries to take advantage of these enhancements, but Adobe strongly recommends deactivating the Use Navigation Services option:

- Choose > Edit > Preferences > General > Display. Deselect the option.

Adobe certification

The Adobe Training and Certification Programs are designed to help Adobe customers improve and promote their product proficiency skills. The Adobe Certified Expert (ACE) program is designed to recognize the high-level skills of expert users. Adobe Certified Training Providers (ACTP) use only Adobe Certified Experts to teach Adobe software classes. Available in either ACTP classrooms or on site, the ACE program is the best way to master Adobe products. For Adobe Certified Training Programs information, visit the Partnering with Adobe Web site at partners.adobe.com.

A Quick Tour of Adobe GoLive

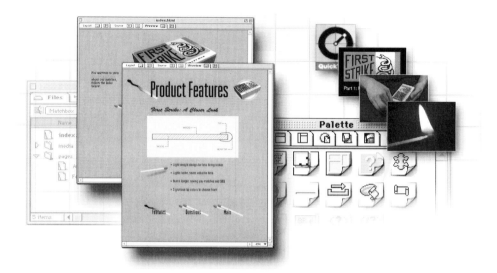

This interactive tour introduces you to key features of Adobe GoLive. During the tour, you'll create a Web site that includes a home page and two linked pages. The pages incorporate formatted text, GIF images, rollovers, JavaScript, and even animation.

For detailed instructions on how to use the features introduced in this tour, see the *Adobe GoLive 4.0 User Guide*. For further lessons on using Adobe GoLive, continue this tour and see the rest of this book.

Important: Before starting Adobe GoLive, make sure that you have installed a copy of the QuickTime 3 plug-in into Adobe GoLive's Plugins (Windows) or Plug-ins (Mac OS) folder. Without this plug-in, you cannot preview QuickTime movies in Adobe GoLive.

The tour takes about an hour to complete. If needed, copy the Tour folder onto your hard drive, so that you can save files in the folder.

Getting started

You'll begin this tour by using your Web browser to view a copy of the finished Web site.

1 Start a Web browser, such as Netscape® Communicator™ or Microsoft Internet Explorer™ 4.0.

Note: Some features of the Web pages you'll view require browsers that support JavaScript and Dynamic Hypertext Markup Language (DHTML). If you don't have an appropriate Web browser, you can use Adobe GoLive to preview some elements of the site. For more information, see "Previewing Web pages with Adobe GoLive" on page 23.

2 Open index.html, the home page of the site:

• In Windows, the path is Tour/TEnd/Matchbox Folder/Matchbox/index.html.

Important: In Windows, your preferences may be set to hide file extensions for known file types. In this case, the files cat.gif, cat.jpg, and cat.html would all display as cat when using the Explorer. In addition, you may have preferences set to hide certain files, such as plug-ins and modules, which are used by Adobe GoLive. See the documentation that came with your system for information on how to display file extensions and show all files. Otherwise, filenames referred to in some steps may be difficult to follow.

• In Mac OS, the path is Tour/TEnd/Matchbox ƒ /Matchbox/index.html.

3 Click the links in the index.html Web page, and explore the site.

4 When you have finished viewing the Web site, quit the browser.

Creating a new site

Now you'll begin creating your own Web site.

1 Start Adobe GoLive.

One or more palettes and a context-sensitive toolbar appear, and (depending on how your preferences are set) an empty document named Untitled.html opens in the document window. The document window can display the document in different views, from raw HTML code to browser-specific previews. Currently, the document is in Layout view. This is the view you will use to edit your pages.

2 If you are using Windows, dock the toolbar to the menu bar in the application window.

Because Adobe GoLive provides a blank home page as part of the site you'll create, you don't need this empty, untitled page for the tour.

3 If it's currently open, close the page Untitled.html. You are now ready to create a new, empty Web site.

4 Choose File > New Site > Blank.

5 Locate and select the Tour folder you copied to your desktop. (In Windows, click the Browse button and use the pop-up dialog box to do this.)

6 Type **Matchbox** in the New Site text box. This will be the name of the folder that contains the site. Then select Create Folder. This creates a grouping folder (in this case, called Matchbox Folder in Windows and Matchbox *f* in Mac OS) that contains the Matchbox site folder plus a special data folder and site document used by Adobe GoLive to manage the site.

Note: *If you are using a system earlier than Mac OS 8.5, press the tab key three times so that the New Site Name text box is highlighted and retype the name. You can also click Cancel to close the dialog box, choose Edit > Preferences > General > Display, deselect Use Navigation Services, click OK, and redo steps 4 through 6.*

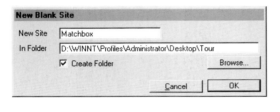

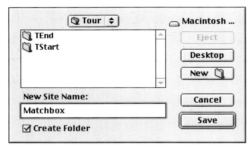

7 Click OK (Windows) or Save or Choose (Mac OS) to create the new Web site.

Adobe GoLive displays a site window, with a home page file, called index.html, already in place. The site window lets you manage Web pages and resources in your Web site. The Files tab of the site window shows the file structure of the site.

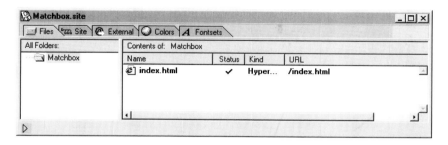

8 Use the Windows Explorer (Windows) or Finder (Mac OS) to open the newly created grouping folder inside the Tour folder, Matchbox Folder (Windows) or Matchbox ƒ (Mac OS), and examine its contents.

Matchbox Folder (Windows) or Matchbox *f* (Mac OS) contains the following folders and files:

• The Matchbox folder stores the Web pages and media that make up your Web site. To upload the site, you upload this folder. Its contents appear in the Files tab of the site window. When you create a new site it already contains a blank home page, whose filename is index.html.

By convention, the home page of a Web site is named index.html. This is the page displayed when a visitor views the site but does not enter the filename of a specific page in the site. For example, if you upload the Matchbox folder to the Web location www.FirstStrikeMatches.com, a visitor who uses a browser to go to http://www.First-StrikeMatches.com/Matchbox would see the file index.html contained in Matchbox.

• The Matchbox.data folder stores stationery and other items Adobe GoLive uses to help you build and maintain your site, but that don't need to be uploaded as part of the site.

• The Matchbox.site (Windows) or Matchbox.π (Mac OS) document is used by Adobe GoLive to record the structure of your Web site so that you can manage the contents of the site in the Files tab of the site window. Opening the Matchbox.site/Matchbox.π document by double-clicking it or using the Open command displays the site window in Adobe GoLive. The document is not uploaded as part of the Web site.

Dragging and dropping to add files to a Web site

You are now ready to add some structure and elements to your Web site by dragging and dropping files. First, you'll add a folder of images and other media files. This will be the source of the images and media you'll add to your Web pages.

1 Using Windows Explorer (Windows) or the Finder (Mac OS), select the Tour/TStart/Media folder, and drag it from the desktop into the Files tab of the site window.

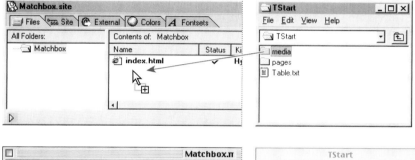

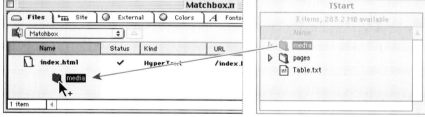

Although you can work from your system's desktop, the site window lets you manage the files from within Adobe GoLive.

2 Open the Media folder in the site window to display the folder's contents:

• In Windows, double-click the Media folder in the site window.

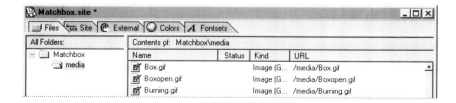

• In Mac OS, click the arrow next to the Media folder icon in the site window.

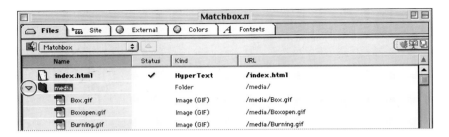

Next, you'll add a new folder to the site. This folder will hold the Web pages you'll create.

3 Create a new folder:

• In Windows, click to select Matchbox in the left pane of the site window. Then choose Site > New > Group to create the folder.

• In Mac OS, choose Site > New > Group to create the folder.

4 Select the new untitled folder in the site window and rename it **Pages**.

Most Web servers are case-sensitive and restrict the characters you can use in filenames and folder names. Don't use a forward slash (/), empty space, or ampersand (&). Don't use a period (.) except as part of an extension (for example, index.html), and don't use the hyphen (-) as the first character in a filename or folder name. Your Web server may have additional requirements.

Your Web site now consists of a file named index.html (the home page of your Web site) as well as two folders: the Media folder you dragged over containing several image files and the Pages folder you created which is currently empty.

Designing a Web page

You'll begin designing your first Web page by opening the home page index.html, listed in the site window.

1 Open the Web page index.html:

• In Windows, select the folder Matchbox in the site window. Then double-click index.html.

• In Mac OS, double-click index.html in the site window.

For easy access to the various windows and palettes in Adobe GoLive, you can set up the document window above the site window, and place the palettes to the side. In Mac OS, you can minimize a palette to an icon by control-clicking the title bar of the palette or dragging it to the right edge of the desktop. To reopen a minimized palette in Mac OS, click the icon. In Windows, you can dock a palette by dragging or double-clicking its title bar and undock it by double-clicking the double lines at the top of the palette. In addition, you can place the document window over the site window and click the Toggle Between Windows button (   ) in the toolbar to switch between the windows.

First, you'll change the title of the Web page. This is the text that appears in the title bar of a Web browser when your page is viewed.

2 Select the text "Welcome to Adobe GoLive 4" located next to the Page icon (   ) at the top of the document window. Replace this text with the new title **First Strike Matches**.

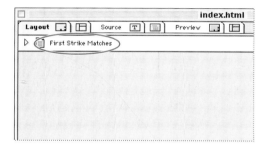

Laying out pages and adding text

One of the objects you'll use often is the *layout grid*. By putting a layout grid on a Web page, you can place objects on the page with one-pixel accuracy. You don't have to use a layout grid that runs the entire length of the page. In fact, using layout grids is optional on a page-by-page basis, but it is often much more convenient to do so.

The grid automatically lengthens to accommodate the objects you place on it. You can also resize the grid by selecting it and dragging a handle or specifying a precise size. The layout grid is one of the many objects available in the palette that you can use to add elements to Web pages.

1 If necessary, Choose View > Palette (Windows) or Window > Palette (Mac OS) to display the Palette. Make sure the Basic tab (   ) is selected in the Palette.

2 Drag the Layout Grid icon from the Palette to your Web page.

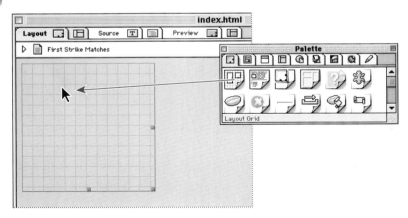

💡 *To display the name of any item in the toolbar or in the Palette, hold the mouse pointer over the item. The name of a button in the toolbar or a tab in the Palette appears next to the pointer. The name of an icon within the Palette appears at the bottom of the Palette.*

You can type directly onto a Web page you are creating in Adobe GoLive without using a layout grid. However, in this tour you'll place a container called a layout text box onto the layout grid. You can then enter text into the layout text box, resize the box, and move it around the grid to easily format the look and placement of the text on your page.

3 Drag the Layout Text Box icon from the Palette to the left side of the layout grid on the Web page.

4 To reposition the layout text box (or any object), deselect it and move the mouse pointer to any of its edges. When the pointer turns into a hand, drag the layout text box to where you want it.

Note: *You can also select an object and move it one pixel at a time by holding down Ctrl+Alt (Windows) or Option (Mac OS) and pressing an arrow key.*

5 Click inside the layout text box and type **Welcome to First Strike Matches**.

6 Press Enter to create a second paragraph and type: **For answers to your burning questions about our matches, use the links below.**

As in a word processor, you can edit and format the text.

7 Select the text "Welcome to First Strike Matches" in the layout text box.

8 In the toolbar, click the Align Center (![Align Center icon]) and Bold (**B**) buttons and choose 6 from the Font Size menu (![Font Size menu]).

9 To resize the layout text box (or any object), move the pointer to one of its handles. When the pointer turns into a hollow (not black) arrow, drag the handle until the box is the size you want.

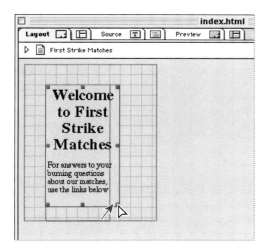

💡 *When designing Web pages, you'll usually want to make them no wider than your visitor's screen. You can choose 580 from the menu at the bottom right of the document window to display the current page at 580 pixels wide, the standard default width for 14-inch monitors. This helps prevent you from adding objects that are too wide to display on a standard page, such as large graphic banners.*

Note: *In Windows, Adobe GoLive creates new pages 520 pixels wide by default. Change the width of these pages to 580 pixels.*

It is good practice to save your project regularly as you work.

10 Choose File > Save.

Adding color

Now you'll add color to the text you entered and to the background of the page.

1 Drag to select the text "Welcome to First Strike Matches" you entered in the Web page.

2 If necessary, choose View > Color Palette (Windows) or Window > Color Palette (Mac OS) to display the Color Palette.

The Color Palette has several tabs representing different color spaces. The tab most often used is for the Web-safe (also called "browser-safe") colors. It's a good idea to use Web-safe colors, because they keep your colors from dithering (shifting) when viewed on platforms that can't display those colors.

3 Click the Web-safe tab ( ) in the Color Palette.

4 Select a color using the grid of sample swatches, the list, or by entering a value in the Value text box. (We chose the color labeled #FF6633.)

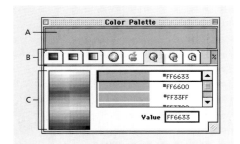

A. Preview pane B. Color space tabs C. Swatches

5 Drag the color from the preview pane at the top of the Color Palette to the selected text in the Web page. Then click away from the text on the Web page to see the result.

Now you'll change the background color of your page.

6 Select a color on the Color Palette for the background. (We chose the color labeled #66CCCC.)

7 Drag the color from the preview pane at the top of the Color Palette to the Page icon
(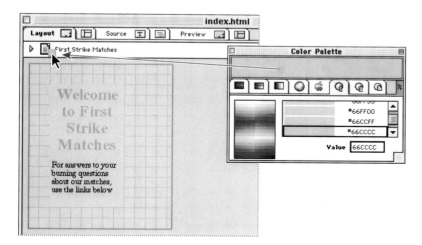) near the top left corner of the document window.

8 Choose File > Save.

Adding images

To make your Web page more visually appealing, you can use images in your design. In
this part of the tour, you'll add three images to the page. You'll add each image by putting
an image placeholder on the page and then linking the placeholder to an image file.

The standard image formats for the Web are Graphical Interchange Format (GIF) and
Joint Photographic Experts Group (JPEG). GIF images are typically used for line art and
JPEGs are typically used for photographs and other images with more than 256 colors. In
this tour, you'll use GIF images.

You'll begin by putting an image placeholder on the page.

1 Drag the Image icon from the Palette and place it on the layout grid to the right of the layout text box on your Web page. (If there isn't enough room, select the layout grid and drag one of its handles to enlarge it.)

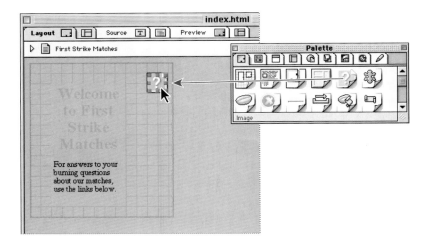

Adobe GoLive provides a context-sensitive palette called the Inspector. This palette lets you quickly customize objects without using commands in the menu bar. You'll use it now to work with the image placeholder.

2 If necessary, choose View > Inspector (Windows) or Window > Inspector (Mac OS) to display the Inspector.

Because an image placeholder is selected, the Inspector appears as the Image Inspector. The Source text box in the Image Inspector states "Empty Reference!" because the image placeholder in your Web page does not refer to an image yet.

Now you'll "point and shoot" to connect the placeholder on the Web page with an image file in the site window.

3 Drag from the Point and Shoot button (⬚) in the Image Inspector to the file Matchbox.gif in the Media folder in the site window.

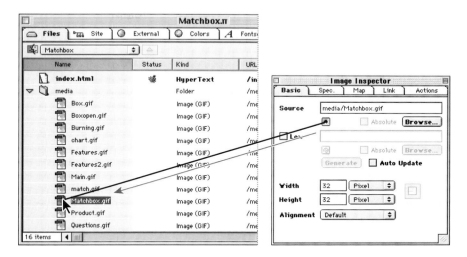

You can tell you've made the connection when the line from the Point and Shoot button connects with and highlights the filename in the site window.

The GIF image now appears on the Web page, and the Source text box in the Image Inspector shows the relative path of the image.

4 To lengthen the layout grid to place more images, click the grid so that the Inspector changes to the Layout Grid Inspector. Enter **360** for Height and click the Enter button (⬚) on the Layout Grid Inspector or press Enter on your keyboard.

5 Drag two more Image icons from the Palette and place them next to each other near the bottom of the layout grid on the page. You can move other objects on the page if they are in the way.

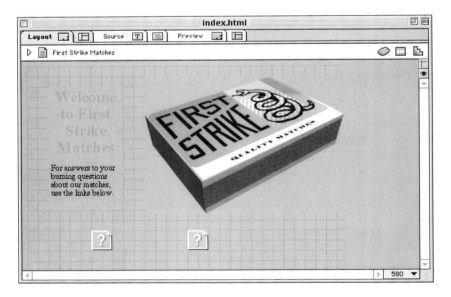

6 Select the empty image placeholder on the left and use the Image Inspector to link it to the file Features.gif in the site window.

💡 *You can also hold down Ctrl+Alt (Windows) or Command (Mac OS) and drag from the image placeholder on a Web page to a file in the site window. This has the same effect as using the Point and Shoot button in the Inspector.*

7 Select the remaining image placeholder and link it to the file Questions.gif.

Now you'll align the two images.

8 Shift-click to select both of the images.

The Inspector changes to the Multiselection Inspector.

9 Click the Align Top button in the Multiselection Inspector to align the tops of both images. (This button is dimmed if the images are already aligned.)

10 Click the Special tab in the Multiselection Inspector. In the Horizontal section, select Offset, enter a distance in pixels (we chose 60), and click the Equidistant Edges button.

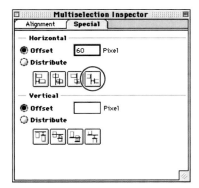

11 Click the Align Center button ( ) in the toolbar to center the buttons.

12 Choose File > Save.

Adding keywords

Adobe GoLive lets you add keywords to a Web page. This nondisplaying text is used by search engines to identify the topics on your page. You'll add keywords to your home page next.

1 Click the triangle next to the Page icon (▤) in the document window to display the head section pane.

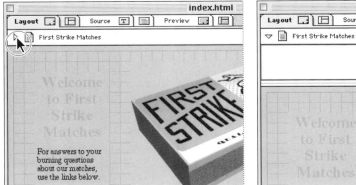

2 Click the Head tab (▤) in the Palette (the third tab from the left).

 3 Drag the Keywords icon from the Palette to the head section pane of the document window.

The Inspector changes to the Keywords Inspector.

4 Enter a word or phrase you want to use as a keyword in the text box at the bottom of the Keywords Inspector. (We used the phrase "First Strike Matches.")

5 Click Add, click the Enter button (▣) in the Keywords Inspector, or press Enter on the keyboard.

6 Enter more words and phrases if you want.

7 When you are done, click the triangle next to the Page icon to close the head section pane.

8 Choose File > Save.

Previewing Web pages with Adobe GoLive

You have just completed your first Web page design with Adobe GoLive. You can preview your page within Adobe GoLive or by using your browser. Here, you'll use Adobe GoLive to preview the page.

💡 *Not all objects on a Web page can be previewed in Adobe GoLive. For example, Adobe GoLive cannot show certain JavaScript actions, anchors, and animations. For this reason, it is always a good idea to preview pages using a Web browser as well.*

1 In the document window, click the Layout Preview tab (▦) (the tab labeled Preview).

The Inspector changes to the Document Layout Controller. You can use this palette to define which browser and which platform you want to emulate in the preview. Defining a different platform is especially useful, because fonts on Web pages usually display larger in Windows than in Mac OS.

2 Choose a browser option from the Root menu in the Document Layout Controller— for example, "Explorer 4 (Windows)" to preview how your page would look in Internet Explorer 4 on a Windows platform. Switch between the different Root menu options and notice how your page changes in Preview view.

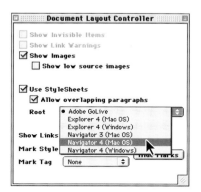

3 When you're through previewing the page, click the Layout Preview tab (▦) in the document window to return to Layout view.

Now you'll set up a Web browser for viewing pages.

4 Choose Edit > Preferences. Then select Browsers from the list in the left pane of the Preferences dialog box to display preferences for browsers.

5 Click Find All to search for Web browsers on your system.

6 Select the browsers you want from the list in the right pane of the dialog box and click OK.

7 Choose a browser by clicking the small triangle that indicates the Browser menu (🖼 ▾) in the toolbar. The browser displays the current page, index.html.

8 Close the page index.html in Adobe GoLive.

Creating a second Web page

You're now ready to create a second Web page for the site. When you are finished, this page will contain formatted text, an example of JavaScript, and a QuickTime movie.

1 Choose File > New to create a new, empty Web page.

2 Select the text "Welcome to Adobe GoLive 4" located next to the Page icon (📄) at the top of the document window. Replace this with the new title **Burning Questions**.

Now you'll change the background color of the page.

3 Select a color on the Color Palette for the background. (We chose the color labeled #66CCCC.)

4 Drag the color from the preview pane in the Color Palette to the Page icon.

5 Choose File > Save to save the page. Name the document Questions.html and save the page inside the Pages folder you created for your site (Tour/Matchbox Folder/Matchbox/Pages in Windows or Tour/Matchbox ƒ /Matchbox/Pages in Mac OS).

Copying design elements from one page to another

To help you design this page, you'll copy the elements from another page as a model.

1 Choose File > Open.

2 Locate and open the file Sample.html located in the Tour/TStart/Pages folder.

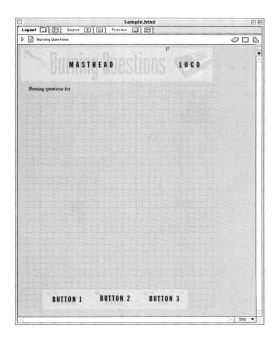

3 Choose Edit > Select All. Then choose Edit > Copy to copy all of its contents.

4 Close the page Sample.html.

5 Select the page Questions.html and choose Edit > Paste to paste the contents into that page.

The images in Questions.html are still linked back to image files in the Tour/TStart/Pages/SampleMedia folder. Now, you'll link them to images in your Matchbox/Media folder.

6 Select the Masthead image in Questions.html.

7 Hold down Ctrl+Alt (Windows) or Command (Mac OS) and drag from the Masthead image placeholder to Burning.gif in the site window. (Remember, this is a shortcut for using the Point and Shoot button in the Image Inspector.) The temporary artwork is replaced with the specific artwork for your Matchbox site.

8 Select the Logo image in the Web page.

The Inspector changes to the Button Inspector.

9 Click the Main icon in the Button Inspector and drag from the Point and Shoot button (⊚) to Box.gif in the site window.

10 Scroll down if necessary to display the images at the bottom of Questions.html.

11 Link the Button 1 image to Features.gif in the site window.

12 Link the Button 2 image to Questions.gif in the site window.

13 Link the Button 3 image to Main.gif in the site window.

You now have linked the images for your page.

14 Choose File > Save.

15 Select the site window.

16 Click the Update button (✔) in the toolbar to establish the new links and update your site with this page.

Adding a table and importing text

Instead of using a layout text box, you'll use a table to format text on this page. This will give you more control over the spacing between paragraphs. And rather than type in all the text, you'll import it.

1 Click the Basic tab of the Palette.

 2 Drag the Table icon from the Palette below the text "Burning questions for" on the page.

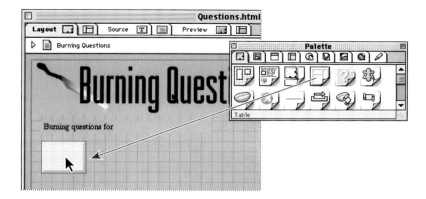

The Inspector changes to the Table Inspector.

3 With the table still selected, enter **450** for Width in the Table Inspector to make the table wider.

4 Click Browse in the Table Inspector to locate the text file you want to import.

5 Select the file Table.txt located in the Tour/TStart folder.

6 For Col. (Column) Separator, choose Tab. Then click Open to import the file into the table.

Notice that the text is separated into multiple rows in the leftmost column. You'll delete the extra columns now and format the table.

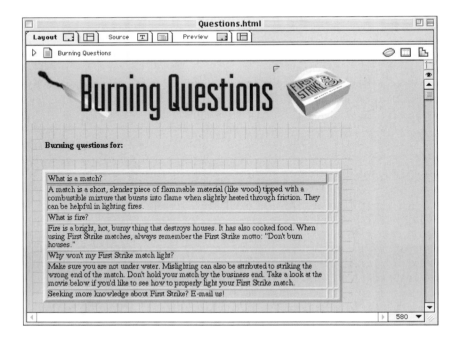

7 In the Table tab of the Table Inspector, enter **1** for Columns.

8 Enter **0** for Border to remove the table border so you display just the text.

9 Enter **5** for Cell Pad to add 5 pixels of extra space around text in the table cells.

10 Select the text "What is a match?" in the first row of the table. Then choose 5 from the Font Size menu (3) in the toolbar so that the text looks like a heading.

11 Select the text "What is Fire?" and "Why won't my First Strike match light?" in turn and change their font size to 5 as well.

12 Choose File > Save.

Adding JavaScript

Now you'll add a simple JavaScript to the page. Adobe GoLive includes a full JavaScript editor. For this tour, you'll add a JavaScript file that shows the date and time.

1 Click to insert the cursor after "Burning questions for."

2 Drag the JavaScript icon from the Palette into the layout text box. The JavaScript placeholder now appears at the end of the phrase.

The Inspector changes to the Body Script Inspector.

3 Click the button next to the Source text box to display the Point and Shoot button ( ).

4 Drag from the Point and Shoot button to the JavaScript file Date.scpt in the Media folder in the site window.

Adding a QuickTime movie

You can place any multimedia element that Netscape Navigator or Microsoft Internet Explorer supports into a Web page you are creating with Adobe GoLive. Here, you'll add a QuickTime movie to the page.

1 If necessary, scroll to display the area below the table and above the match images on the Web page. Then drag the Plug-in icon from the Palette to this area.

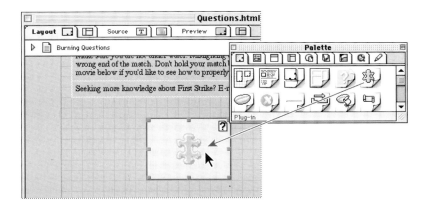

The Inspector changes to the Plug-in Inspector. Now you'll connect the Plug-in placeholder on the Web page to a QuickTime file in the site window.

Note: *The QuickTime 3 plug-in must be installed in Adobe GoLive's Plugins (Windows) or Plug-ins (Mac OS) folder for the QuickTime preview to work.*

2 With the placeholder selected on the Web page, drag from the Point and Shoot button in the Plug-in Inspector to the QuickTime file Strike.mov in the Media folder in the site window.

The title Strike now appears in the placeholder on the Web page and the Inspector changes to the Folder Inspector.

3 Reselect the Plug-in placeholder to change the Inspector to the Plug-in Inspector.

4 Click the QuickTime tab of the Plug-in Inspector.

5 Select Show Controller to display a movie control bar when visitors play the movie.

6 Deselect Autoplay so the movie doesn't start until a visitor chooses to play it.

7 With the Plug-in placeholder still selected, click the Align Center button (⊡) in the toolbar to center align the movie to the layout grid. (This button is dimmed if the movie is already aligned to the center.)

8 Choose File > Save.

9 Do one of the following:

• Choose a browser from the Browser menu (🖼 ▾) in the toolbar. The browser displays Questions.html and you can view the JavaScript date and time and play the movie.

• Click the Preview tab in the document window to play the movie (although you cannot view the JavaScript date and time).

10 In Adobe GoLive, close the page Questions.html.

Adding a predesigned Web page and animating it

In this section of the tour, you'll add an existing Web page to your site and make the page's content more dynamic by adding rollovers and animation.

1 Move the predesigned page:

• In Windows, use Windows Explorer to drag the Web page Features.html from the Tour/TStart/Pages folder into the Tour/Matchbox Folder/Matchbox/Pages folder. (Do not drag it to the site window.)

• In Mac OS, use the Finder to drag the Web page Features.html from the Tour/TStart/Pages folder into the Tour/Matchbox ƒ /Matchbox/Pages folder. (Do not drag it to the site window.)

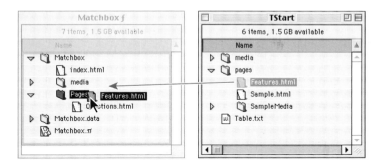

When you dragged the page Sample.html into the site window earlier in the tour, Adobe GoLive updated the links so that they still referred to the original images in the Tour/TStart/Pages/SampleMedia folder. That is why you needed to relink the images to files in the Tour/Matchbox Folder/Media folder (Windows) or Tour/Matchbox ƒ /Media folder (Mac OS).

This time, by moving the page Features.html from one folder to another without dragging it into the site window, the links are not updated. Instead, the page is looking for images in a Media folder one level above its current location. Because Tour/Matchbox Folder/Matchbox/Media (Windows) or Tour/Matchbox ƒ /Matchbox/Media (Mac OS) contains the appropriate images, once you update the site, the correct images will appear in the page Features.html without any relinking.

2 Open the Pages folder in the site window.

3 Click the Update button (☑) in the toolbar to update the site window with the new page. The new page Features.html now appears in the site window.

4 Double-click Features.html in the site window to open the page.

Creating rollovers in Adobe GoLive

Here you will make a rollover on the page. Rollovers are objects that change their look as you move the mouse pointer over or click them.

To save time, a button image placeholder has already been added to the page from the Palette and a GIF image of a closed matchbox has been linked to the placeholder.

1 Click to select the image of the matchbox.

Notice that the Inspector changes to the Button Inspector. Notice, too, that the Main icon is selected in the Button Inspector. This indicates the button image placeholder is linked to the file Box.gif, the image you want to display when the mouse pointer is away from the button.

Now you'll select the image that will appear when a visitor's pointer is over the button on the Web page.

2 Click the Over icon in the Button Inspector. Then click the button next to the text box to activate the Point and Shoot button (▣).

3 Drag from the Point and Shoot button to Boxopen.gif in Media folder in the site window.

Because you are in Layout view, the button on the Web page still shows the Main image for the rollover. However, the appropriate image is shown in the Over icon in the Button Inspector.

4 Choose File > Save.

5 Choose a browser from the Browser menu ( ) in the toolbar. The browser displays Features.html and you can move the mouse pointer over the button to preview your rollover.

6 When you are through, select the Features.html document window in Adobe GoLive.

Animating a page

HTML 4.0 adds Dynamic Hypertext Markup Language (DHTML) to the options you can use in creating a Web page. With DHTML, you can add movable, stackable layers called floating boxes that can move across a Web page, animating your site. These floating boxes can contain text, images, and even JavaScript. In this part of the tour, you'll animate the page with a graphic in a floating box.

Note: Only HTML 4.0-compatible browsers such as Microsoft Internet Explorer 4.0 and Netscape Communicator can display DHTML animations.

To save you time, the floating box placeholder has already been added to the page from the Palette, an image placeholder has been put inside it, and a GIF image of a match has been connected to the image placeholder.

You can now give motion to the floating box so it moves from item to item in the list when a visitor views the page.

1 Click an edge of the floating box to select it. Make sure the floating box is selected and not just the image within it. The floating box is selected when the pointer changes to a hand pointed to the left. (If the hand is pointed up, the image is selected and not the floating box.)

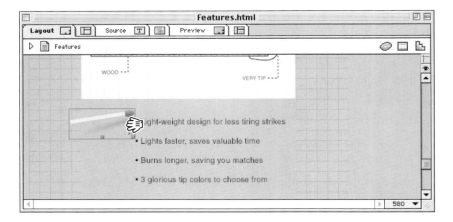

The Inspector changes to the Floating Box Inspector.

2 Click the Record button (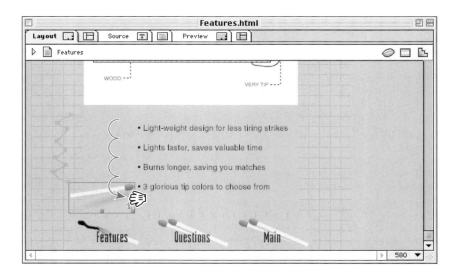) in the Floating Box Inspector to begin recording.

3 Move the pointer over the floating box so that the hand points to the left, then drag the floating box around the Web page. (We moved the box so the match pointed from feature to feature in the list.) Then release the mouse button to stop the recording.

4 Choose File > Save.

5 Click the Preview tab (▢) in the document window to view the finished motion.

6 Click the Layout tab (▢) in the document window to return to Layout view when you are done.

7 Close the page.

Creating links

You now have three pages with varying amounts of content. But as yet, there's no way visitors to your site can get from one page to the other. The next thing to do is to add links that connect the pages.

First, you will link the text in the index.html page so that visitors can click there to go to the other two pages.

1 Double-click index.html in the site window to open that page for editing.

2 In index.html, select the text "burning questions."

The Inspector changes to the Text Inspector.

3 Click the New Link button (▢) in the toolbar.

4 Drag from the Point and Shoot button (▣) in the Text Inspector to the Web page Questions.html in the Pages folder in the site window. Then click away from the text to deselect it.

The text in index.html is now blue and underlined to indicate it is a link. You have just created your first link in Adobe GoLive.

5 Choose File > Save.

6 Click the Preview tab (▢) in the document window to view the page.

7 Click the "burning questions" text to try out the new link.

In Windows, Questions.html replaces index.html in the document window. In Mac OS, Questions.html opens in a new document window on top of index.html.

8 Do one of the following:

• In Windows, where Questions.html replaced index.html in the document window, click the Layout tab (▢) in the document window to return to index.html in Layout view.

• In Mac OS, where Questions.html opened as a separate page, close it so that only index.html is open.

Linking from images

In addition to linking from text, you can also link from a graphic. Here you will link the buttons you created in the index.html page to the Features.html and Questions.html pages.

1 Click the Layout tab (▢) in the document window, if necessary, to return the index.html to Layout view.

2 Select the Features image on index.html.

The Inspector changes to the Image Inspector.

3 Click the Link tab in the Image Inspector.

4 Click the New Link button (▢) on the Image Inspector. This is the same as clicking the New Link button in the toolbar.

5 Drag from the Point and Shoot button (▢) in the Image Inspector to the Web page Features.html in the site window.

The image has a bright blue border around it indicating that it's a link. You'll remove this border because it's already clear the button is a link. In addition, the Inspector changes to the Folder Inspector.

6 Reselect the image to change the Inspector to the Image Inspector.

7 Click the Spec. (Special) tab in the Image Inspector. Then select Border to give the image a border of 0 width.

8 Select the Questions image on the Web page. Then create a link for it and remove its blue border using the same steps you used for the Features image, but this time link Questions to the Web page Questions.html in the site window.

9 Choose File > Save.

10 Click the Preview tab (▢) in the document window to view the page.

11 Click the Features link to open the page Features.html.

12 Do one of the following:

• In Windows, click the Layout tab (▢) in the document window to return to index.html in Layout view. Then click the Questions link to open the page Questions.html.

• In Mac OS, click the Questions link to open the page Questions.html.

13 Close all open pages.

Creating e-mail links

Now you'll add a link to the Questions.html page that brings up an e-mail window with an e-mail address in it.

1 Double-click Questions.html in the site window to open the page.

2 Click the External tab (⊙) in the site window.

The External tab lets you store nonfile objects, such as URLs and e-mail addresses. Here, you'll use the External tab to store an e-mail address.

3 Click the Site tab (⊞) (the fifth tab from the left) in the Palette. This tab contains elements for sites, such as pages, URLs, and e-mail addresses.

4 Drag the Address icon from the Palette to the site window.

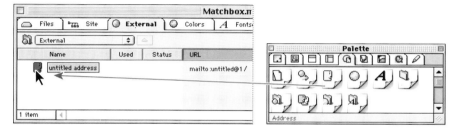

5 Double-click the Address icon in the site window to change the Inspector to the Reference Inspector.

6 In the Name text box of the Reference Inspector, enter a name for the address. For example, change "untitled address" to "Anne's Address." Although it's not required, entering names helps you manage addresses in a site.

7 In the URL text box, enter an e-mail address after "mailto:". For example, change "mailto:untitled@1/" to "mailto:AnneSmith@mycompany.com". Make sure that you leave "mailto:" in the text box and that there are no spaces between it and the e-mail address.

8 Select the text "E-mail us" at the bottom of the list of questions in the Questions.html page.

9 Click the New Link button (⊑⊒) in the toolbar.

The link is highlighted and underlined. Now you can attach the text as a link to the e-mail address you just created.

10 Drag from the Point and Shoot button ( ) in the Text Inspector to the Address icon in the site window.

11 Choose File > Save.

12 Choose a Web browser from the Browser menu ( ) in the toolbar. Then use the Questions.html page displayed in the browser to click the e-mail link and display an e-mail editor.

13 Close the page Questions.html in Adobe GoLive.

To save you time in the tour, the remaining links have already been provided.

Managing sites

Now you'll change the name of a file and update the links to it, so you can learn how to manage a site in Adobe GoLive.

1 Click the Files tab of the site window.

2 Select the filename Questions.html in the site window and change it to Answers.html.

Because changing the name of a file would normally break the links from any pages that were connected to it under its old name, Adobe GoLive displays a dialog box that lets you update all the links affected by the name change.

3 Click OK.

The Link Inspector lets you review all incoming and outgoing links and embedded items, such as images, assigned to a Web page.

4 Select the Web page Answers.html in the site window.

5 Click the Link Inspector button (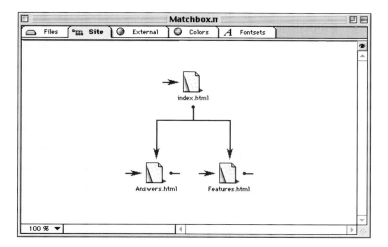) in the toolbar to display all of the links and embedded images assigned to that page.

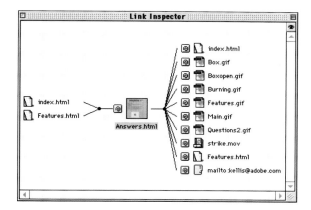

6 Close the Link Inspector.

Adobe GoLive also provides a visual snapshot of your Web site, so you can view how your three pages are related.

7 Click the Site tab in your site window.

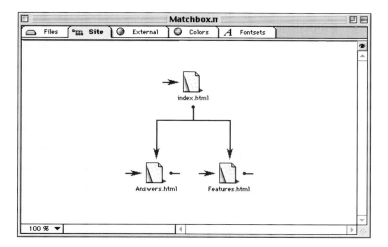

Your Web pages appear with a graphical representation of the link hierarchy of your site—beginning with your home page, index.html. Notice that the Site tab does not show a folder hierarchy as in the Files Tab or in Windows Explorer (Windows) or the Finder (Mac OS). There you would see that Answers.html and Features.html are in the Pages folder.

Previewing and testing files

You have now finished creating a site in Adobe GoLive. Go ahead and preview it using your Web browser.

1 Do one of the following:

• Click the Files tab in the site window. Double-click the page index.html in the site window. Then choose a Web browser from the Browser menu ( ) in the toolbar.

• If necessary, start a Web browser. (If you do not have enough memory to run the browser and Adobe GoLive, quit Adobe GoLive.) Then use the Open or equivalent command in the browser to locate and open the file Tour/Matchbox Folder/Matchbox/index.html in Windows or Tour/Matchbox ƒ /Matchbox/index.html in Mac OS.

• Click the links in the Web page and explore the site you just created.

Lesson 1

1 | Working with Text

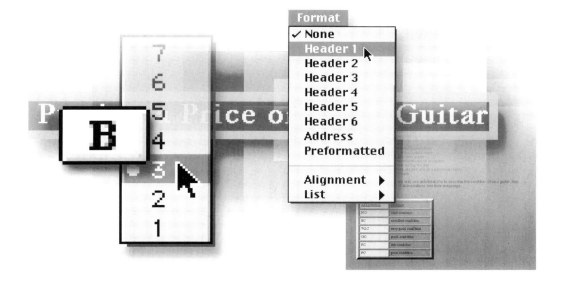

With Adobe GoLive, you can add text to a page using a variety of methods, including typing directly in the document window. Once the text is added, you can easily format it and color it. In addition, you can use a table to control how text wraps on a page, or to present spreadsheet data or other information in rows and columns.

In this lesson, you'll learn how to do the following:

- Add text to a page by typing directly in the document window.
- Apply paragraph and physical styles to text.
- Create numbered and unnumbered lists.
- Add a line break.
- Change the color of text.
- Add tables to a page, and format the tables.
- Use a table to control how text wraps on a page.
- Import data into a table from another application.
- Apply a new set of fonts to the text on a page.
- Preview a Web page in Adobe GoLive.

This lesson will take about 45 minutes to complete.

If needed, copy the Lesson01 folder onto your hard drive. As you work on this lesson, you'll overwrite the Start files. If you need to restore the Start files, copy them from the Adobe GoLive Classroom in a Book CD.

Getting started

In this lesson, you'll work on the design of a Web page for a fictional company called Gage Vintage Guitars. The Web page provides information about how to get your guitar appraised by the company.

First you'll view the finished Web page in your browser.

1 Start your Web browser.

2 Open the Appraise.html file, located inside the Lesson01/01End folder.

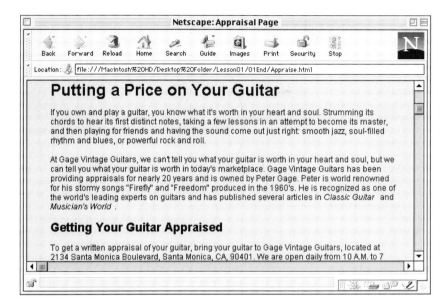

3 When you have finished viewing the page, close Appraise.html and quit your browser.

Designing the Web page

To get you started with the design of the Web page, we've created the page in Adobe GoLive and added some text. You'll open the page.

1 Start Adobe GoLive. A new document named Untitled.html opens.

Setting up your work area

We recommend that you set up your work area as shown in the following illustration. In Windows, dock the toolbar by dragging its title bar directly below the menu bar, and click the Maximize button to maximize the application window. For both platforms, place the document window at the top, the site window at the bottom, and the palettes on the right side of the desktop. (To move a window, drag its title bar.)

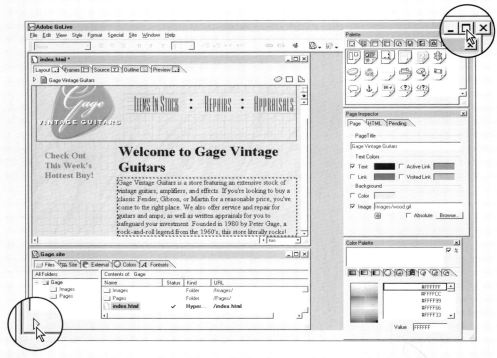

When necessary, click the Aspect Control icon to display the expanded pane of the site window. In Windows, the Aspect Control icon appears as a triangle in the bottom left corner of the site window.

In Mac OS, the Aspect Control icon appears as a bar of images in the upper right corner of the site window.

Windows *You can dock palettes by moving them to the right side of the desktop. However, we recommend that you keep palettes floating on the desktop, so that you can view their titles for easier identification. To float a palette, double-click its title bar.*

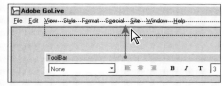 

Drag toolbar to dock it.   *Double-click palette's title bar to float it.*

Mac OS *You can collapse palettes by Ctrl-clicking their title bars or moving them to the right side of the desktop. You can also collapse document windows and the site window by Ctrl-clicking their title bars or moving them to the bottom of the desktop. To expand a palette or window, click its icon.*

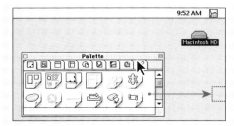 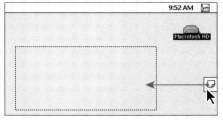

Drag palette to collapse it.   *Drag palette to expand it.*

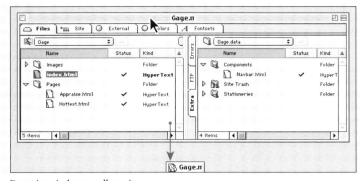

Drag site window to collapse it.

If your workspace is limited, you can keep the site window collapsed and still connect files to placeholders on the page using the Point and Shoot button in the Inspector. Drag from the Point and Shoot button in the Inspector to the site window, and continue to hold down the mouse button. The site window expands, and you can drag to the desired file in the window.

You don't need a new document for this lesson.

2 Choose File > Close to close Untitled.html.

3 Choose File > Open, and open the Appraise.html file, located inside the Lesson01/01Start folder.

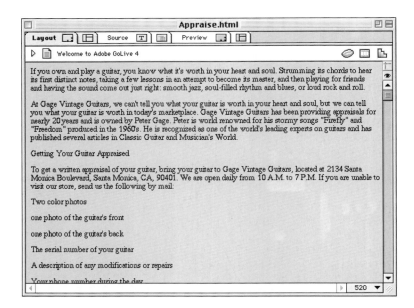

Now you're ready to begin designing the Web page. First you'll change the title of the page. When viewed in a Web browser, the title of the page appears in the title bar of the browser.

4 Select the page title, "Welcome to Adobe GoLive 4."

5 Type **Appraisal Page** as the new title, and click in the blank space beneath the title to deselect it.

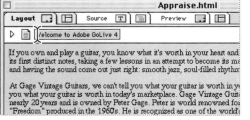

Selecting page title

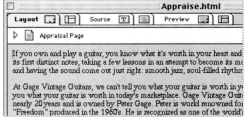

New page title

Now you'll select a default window size for the page.

6 Choose 580 from the Window Size menu in the lower right corner of the document window.

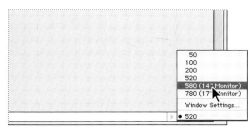

Choosing window size

Now you'll change the background color of the page to khaki.

7 If necessary, choose View > Inspector (Windows) or Window > Inspector (Mac OS) to display the Inspector.

8 Click the Page icon (📄) in the upper left corner of the document window. The Inspector changes to the Page Inspector.

9 In the Page Inspector, make sure that the Page tab is selected. Under Background, click the Color field. The Color Palette displays, if it's not already displayed.

In this lesson, you'll use the Web I tab of the Color Palette, which contains 216 colors that don't dither and are safe for use on the Web across platforms.

10 In the Color Palette, click the Web I tab (🌐). In the Value text box, type **CCCC99**, and press Enter or Return. The selected color appears in the preview pane.

11 Drag the color from the preview pane to the Page icon in the document window.

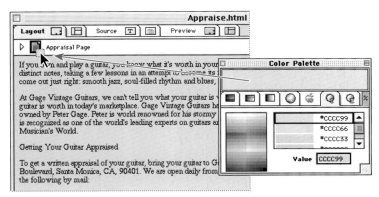

Changing page's background color

The Background Color option in the Page Inspector is automatically selected, and the background color of the page changes to khaki.

12 Choose File > Save to save the page.

Adding text

You can add text to an Adobe GoLive document by typing directly in the document window. Now you'll add a heading to the page.

1 Click before the first word in the document to insert a cursor.

2 Type **Putting a Price on Your Guitar**, and press Enter or Return.

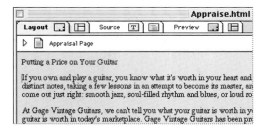

Adobe GoLive provides a variety of additional methods for adding text to your documents:

• You can import text from another application into a table, which you'll do later in this lesson.

• You can add text to a page using layout text boxes and floating boxes, which you'll do in Lesson 2, "Laying Out Web Pages."

• You can copy text from a document created in another application, such as Microsoft Word, and paste the text into an Adobe GoLive document.

• You can drag text clips, created from SimpleText or Note Pad documents, from the desktop to Adobe GoLive documents.

▪ For more information about adding text to Adobe GoLive documents, see "Creating text" in Chapter 4 of the *Adobe GoLive 4.0 User Guide*.

Formatting text

Adobe GoLive lets you format text in a variety of ways. You use paragraph styles, such as Header 1 and Header 2, to format paragraphs. You use physical styles, such as bold and italic, to emphasize text. And you use structural styles, such as Emphasis and Strong, to both emphasize and classify text.

Now you'll apply paragraph styles to format the headings in the document.

1 Click anywhere in the "Putting a Price on Your Guitar" heading on the page.

2 Choose Header 1 from the Paragraph Format menu in the toolbar.

3 Click in the "Getting Your Guitar Appraised" paragraph, and choose Header 2 from the Paragraph Format menu.

Now you'll apply physical styles to some of the text in the document.

4 Select the phrase "Classic Guitar" near the end of the paragraph before the "Getting Your Guitar Appraised" heading.

5 Click the Bold button (**B**) in the toolbar to make the selected text bold.

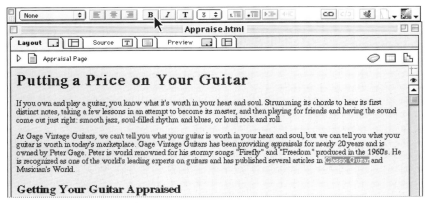

Applying physical (bold) style to text

You can easily remove a physical style and apply a new one.

6 Click the Bold button again to remove the bold style from the selected text.

7 Click the Italic button (*I*) in the toolbar to italicize the selected text, and click in the blank space outside the text to deselect it.

8 Apply the Italic style to the phrase "Musician's World" at the end of the same sentence.

▣ To apply a structural style to selected text, choose an option from the Style > Structure submenu. For more information about structural styles, see "Formatting text using structural tags" in Chapter 4 of the *Adobe GoLive 4.0 User Guide*.

Creating lists

You can use Adobe GoLive to quickly format paragraphs as numbered or unnumbered lists. Now you'll create a numbered list from some of the text on the page.

1 Scroll down to display the "Getting Your Guitar Appraised" section.

2 Select the seven paragraphs below the first paragraph in the section. (Your selection should begin with "Two color photos" and end with "$25 payable by Visa, Mastercard, or a personal check drawn from a US bank.")

3 Click the Numbered List button (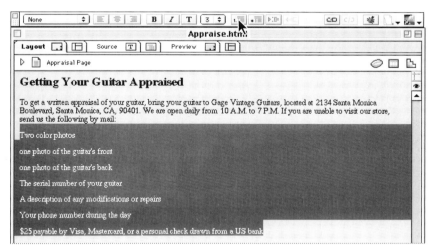) in the toolbar to format the seven paragraphs as a numbered list.

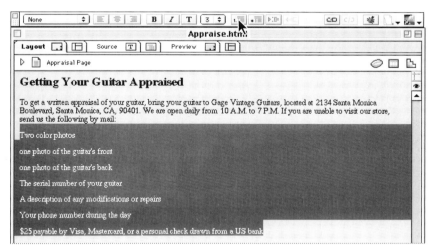

Formatting text as numbered list

By default, Adobe GoLive creates a numbered list with Arabic numerals. You can choose from several options to change the numbering style of the list.

4 Choose Format > List > Upper Roman to change the leading characters to uppercase Roman numerals.

Now you'll change the numbered list into an unnumbered list.

5 Click the Unnumbered List button ( ) in the toolbar to change the leading characters from numbers to bullets.

6 Click in the blank space outside the list to deselect it.

Adobe GoLive lets you easily create a hierarchical list with different numbering styles or leading characters.

7 Select the second and third items in the list.

8 Click the Increase List Level button (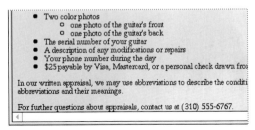) in the toolbar to further indent the selected items and change their leading characters from bullets to circles.

- Two color photos
  - one photo of the guitar's front
  - one photo of the guitar's back
- The serial number of your guitar
- A description of any modifications or repairs
- Your phone number during the day
- $25 payable by Visa, Mastercard, or a personal check drawn fro

In our written appraisal, we may use abbreviations to describe the conditi abbreviations and their meanings.

For further questions about appraisals, contact us at (310) 555-6767.

Indenting list items

You can also use the Increase List Level button to change the indentation of a paragraph on the page.

9 Click the paragraph above the unnumbered list, and click the Increase List Level button twice to indent the paragraph twice.

You can easily return the paragraph to its original indentation.

10 Click the Decrease List Level button (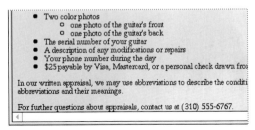) in the toolbar twice to remove the indentation from the paragraph.

Adding a line break

Notice that the last item in the unnumbered list is longer than the other items. You can use a line break to make the last item flow onto two lines, rather than one.

1 Click before the word "drawn" in the last item to insert a cursor.

2 If necessary, choose View > Palette (Windows) or Window > Palette (Mac OS) to display the Palette, and make sure that the Basic tab (▣) is selected.

 3 Double-click the Line Break icon in the Palette, or drag the Line Break icon from the Palette to the cursor on the page.

The line breaks, and the text beginning with "drawn" is moved to the following line.

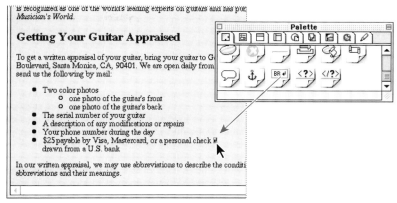

Adding line break

💡 *You can also add a line break by clicking inside a paragraph to insert a cursor and pressing Shift+Enter or Shift+Return.*

Changing the color of text

Now you'll change the color of the unnumbered list to red.

1 Select the text in the unnumbered list, including the leading character of the first item in the list.

2 In the Color Palette, type **990000** in the Value text box, and press Enter or Return. The selected color appears in the preview pane. Drag the color from the preview pane to the selected text on the page.

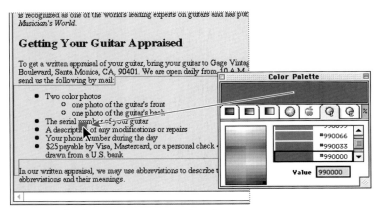

Dragging color from preview pane to selected text

3 Click in the blank space outside the selected text to deselect it.

4 Choose File > Save.

Adding tables

Adobe GoLive lets you quickly add tables to your documents. Tables are often used to control how text wraps on a Web page. They are also used to present information in rows and columns. In this lesson, you'll create and format tables for both purposes.

Adding a table to control how text wraps

To see how text wraps on the page without the use of a table, you'll change the window size of the document.

1 Choose 200 from the Window Size menu in the lower right corner of the document window.

Notice that the text wraps so that all of the text fits inside the smaller window. If you don't want the text to wrap to accommodate a change in window size, you can place the text inside a single-cell table. Text in a single-cell table wraps at the set width of the table, even when the window size changes.

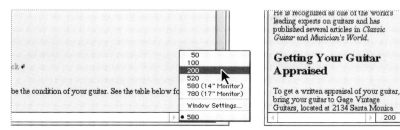

Choosing smaller window size   *Result*

Now you'll add a table to the page, which you'll use to control how text wraps on the page.

2 Choose 580 from the Window Size menu to return to the default window size.

3 Scroll up to bring the beginning of the document into view. Click before the "Putting a Price on Your Guitar" heading on the page to insert a cursor.

You'll insert a table at the cursor location.

4 Double-click the Table icon in the Palette, or drag the Table icon from the Palette to the cursor on the page.

An empty table containing three rows and three columns appears at the cursor location, and the text on the page moves downward. The Inspector changes to the Table Inspector, with the Table tab selected.

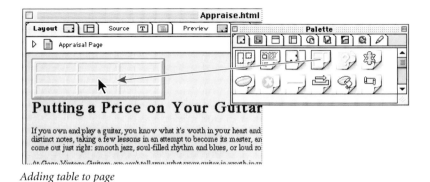

Adding table to page

Now you'll remove rows and columns to create a single-cell table.

5 In the Table Inspector, type **1** for Rows, and click the Enter button (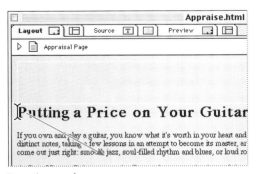) or press Enter or Return. (Whenever the Enter button appears after a text box or field, you must click the button or press Enter or Return on the keyboard to apply the value.)

6 Type **1** for Columns, and press Enter or Return.

Now you'll specify options for the table's appearance.

7 Type **580** for Width, and press Enter or Return to increase the width of the table.

8 Type **0** for Border, and press Enter or Return to remove the table's border. Type **25** for Cell Pad, and press Enter or Return to increase the horizontal and vertical spacing of the table cell.

The Cell Pad option specifies the top, left, right, and bottom margins within each table cell. When you use this option with a single-cell table that contains all of the text on the page, you're essentially specifying margins for the page.

Now you'll drag the text on the page to the table cell.

9 Position the pointer before the "Putting a Price on Your Guitar" heading, and drag to select all of the text on the page.

10 Scroll up to bring the table into view. Position the pointer over the selected text so that the pointer turns into a hand, and drag the selected text to the table cell.

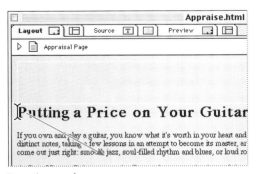
Dragging to select text on page

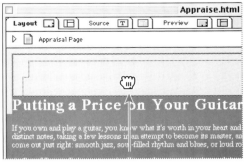
Dragging selected text to table cell

11 Scroll up to bring the beginning of the document into view. Click outside the selected text to deselect it.

Note: In Mac OS, if the main heading loses its paragraph formatting, reapply the Header 1 paragraph format to it.

Now you'll reduce the window size again to see how the text on the page wraps inside a table.

12 Choose 200 from the Window Size menu.

Notice that the text in the table wraps at the set width of the table, even when the window size changes.

13 Choose 580 from the Window Size menu to return to the default window size.

14 Choose File > Save.

Adding a table to present spreadsheet data

In its written appraisals, Gage Vintage Guitars uses abbreviations to describe the condition of a guitar. You'll add a second table to the page that will contain a list of abbreviations used by the company and their meanings. Then you'll import data into the table from a text-only file created in a word-processing application.

1 Scroll down to bring the end of the document into view. Click after the last word in the paragraph beginning with "In our written appraisal," and press Enter or Return.

 2 Double-click the Table icon in the Palette, or drag the Table icon from the Palette to the cursor on the page.

An empty table appears at the cursor location, and the Inspector changes to the Table Inspector.

Notice that you placed the second table within the existing table cell on the page. Adobe GoLive lets you place a variety of objects into table cells, including text, other tables, and images.

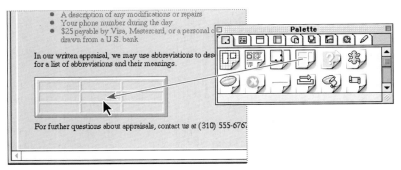

Nesting a table

Now you'll import data into the table from a text-only file containing data separated by tabs. If you have a word-processing application installed on your system, you can open the text-only file to view its contents. If you don't have a word-processing application, skip to step 6.

3 Start your word-processing application.

4 Open the Table.txt file, located inside the Lesson01/01Start folder.

5 When you have finished viewing the file, close it and quit your word-processing application.

6 In the Table Inspector of Adobe GoLive, click the Browse button for the Import Tab-Text option.

7 Select the Table.txt file, located inside the Lesson01/01Start folder. Choose TAB from the Col. (Column) Separator pop-up menu, and click Open.

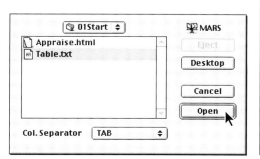

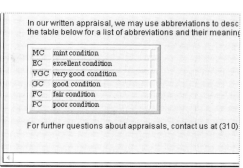

Importing file with tab separator   *Result*

Adobe GoLive adds extra columns and rows to the table as necessary to accommodate the data, and imports the data into the table.

Note: *Most spreadsheet applications can export data to a text-only file containing data separated by tabs. For more information, see the documentation of your spreadsheet application.*

Formatting a table that presents spreadsheet data

Because the third column does not contain data, you'll remove it from the table.

1 In the Table Inspector, type **2** for Columns, and press Enter or Return.

Now you'll specify options for the table's appearance.

2 Choose Auto from the pop-up menu for Width.

3 Type **6** for Border, and press Enter or Return to increase the width of the table's border. Type **4** for Cell Pad, and press Enter or Return to increase the horizontal and vertical spacing of each table cell. Type **4** for Cell Space, and press Enter or Return to increase the space between table cells.

Now you'll add a caption above the table.

4 Select Caption. If the Above Table option isn't already chosen, choose it from the pop-up menu.

5 Click directly above the table to insert a cursor, and type **Abbreviations**.

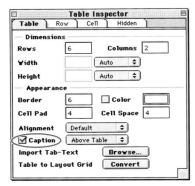

Caption and Above Table options   *Typing "Abbreviations" above table*

6 Click the Left Align button (▤) in the toolbar to align the caption to the left side of the table.

7 Select the "Abbreviations" text, and click the Bold button (**B**) in the toolbar.

♀ *Instead of selecting text by dragging, you can select a single word by double-clicking it or a line of text by triple-clicking it.*

Now you'll increase the font size of the "Abbreviations" text.

You can use the Font Size menu to apply custom font sizes that override the browser's preferences. Most browsers are set to display text at 12 points. The Adobe GoLive Font Size menu contains font sizes from 1 to 7. A font size of 3 displays text at the size set in the browser's preferences, a font size of 2 displays text at one size smaller, and a font size of 4 displays text at one size larger.

8 Choose 4 from the Font Size menu in the toolbar, and click in the blank space outside the caption to deselect it.

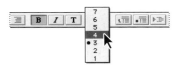

Now you'll add headings to each column of the table. You'll begin by adding an empty row at the beginning of the table.

9 Click the bottom edge of the first cell in the left column of the table to select it. (Make sure that you select the cell, not the text.)

The Cell tab is automatically selected in the Table Inspector.

10 In the Table Inspector, click the Add Row button to add a row above the current selection.

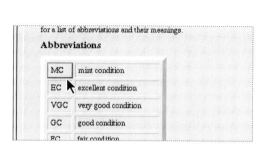

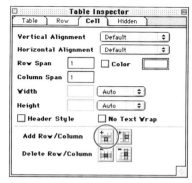

Clicking bottom edge of table cell to select it   *Add Row button*

11 Click inside the new empty, first cell in the left column of the table to insert a cursor.

12 Type **Abbreviation**, press Tab to move the cursor to the first cell in the right column, and type **Meaning**.

Now you'll format the column headings.

13 Select the "Abbreviation" text, and choose Style > Underline to underline it. Then select the "Meaning" text, and underline it.

Now you'll adjust the width of the columns in the table.

14 Click the bottom edge of any cell in the left column of the table to select it.

15 In the Table Inspector, choose Pixel from the menu to the right of the Width text box. For Width, type **100**, and press Enter or Return.

The selected cell and all other cells in its column increase in width.

16 Click the bottom edge of any cell in the right column of the table to select it. Choose Pixel from the menu to the right of the Width text box. For Width, type **140**, and press Enter or Return.

💡 *You can also adjust the width of a table column by positioning the pointer on the right edge of the column so that the pointer turns into a double-headed arrow, and dragging to the left or right.*

17 Choose File > Save.

Changing the color of table cells

Now you'll change the color of the cells in the table to yellow.

1 Move the pointer to the left edge of the table so that the pointer turns into a hand, and click to select the table.

The Table tab is automatically selected in the Table Inspector.

2 In the Color Palette, type **FFFFCC** in the Value text box, and press Enter. The selected color appears in the preview pane. Drag the color from the preview pane to the Color field in the Table Inspector.

The Color option in the Table Inspector is automatically selected, and the color of the table cells changes to yellow.

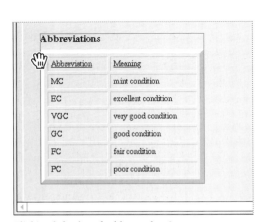

Clicking left edge of table to select it

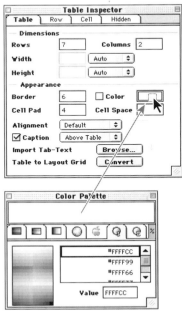

Dragging color from preview pane to Color field in Table Inspector

You can also change the color of individual table cells. You'll change the color of the cells in the right column to green.

3 Shift-click the top of the right column to select all of the cells in the column.

Selecting all cells in column

The Cell tab in the Table Inspector is automatically selected.

4 In the Color Palette, type **99CC99** in the Value text box, and press Enter. The selected color appears in the preview pane. Drag the color from the preview pane to the Color field in the Table Inspector.

The Color option in the Table Inspector is automatically selected, and the color of the selected cells changes to green.

5 Click in the blank space outside the table to deselect all of its cells.

Applying fonts

Adobe GoLive contains default sets of fonts that you can apply to text in your documents. One set contains the Arial, Helvetica, and Geneva fonts. If you use this set for your Web page, a viewer's browser will attempt to display text first in Arial, second in Helvetica, and third in Geneva. If none of the fonts in the set are installed on the viewer's system, the browser displays text using its default font.

Now you'll display the Font Set Editor to learn more about the sets of fonts available for your document.

1 Choose Style > Font > Edit Font Sets to display the Font Set Editor.

2 Display the default sets of fonts:

• In Windows, choose Default Font Sets from the menu in the upper left corner of the dialog box.

- In Mac OS, select Default in the left pane of the dialog box.

3 Select Arial in the Font Sets pane of the dialog box.

The Arial set of fonts appears in the Font Names pane of the dialog box.

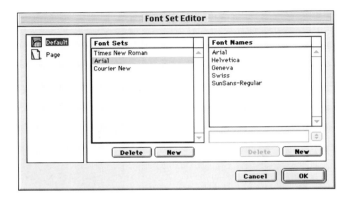

4 Click Cancel to close the dialog box.

Now you'll change the set of fonts used for the text in the document.

5 Choose Edit > Select All to select all of the text in the document.

6 Choose Style > Font > Arial to choose the Arial fonts for the selected text.

7 Click inside the document to deselect the text.

Most of the text in the document changes to the Arial font. Notice that the text in the table continues to use the Times font. To change the fonts used by the text in the table, you first need to select the table caption and cells individually.

8 Select the "Abbreviations" text in the table caption, and choose Style > Font > Arial. Then click outside the selected text to deselect it.

The text in the table caption changes to the Arial font.

9 Shift-click the top of the left column to select all of the cells in the column. Shift-click the top of the right column to add its cells to the selection. Then choose Style > Font > Arial, and click outside the selected table cells to deselect them.

The text in the table cells changes to the Arial font.

🔲 You can also use Adobe GoLive to create sets of fonts that you can apply to text in your documents. For more information, see "Choosing a font set" in Chapter 4 of the *Adobe GoLive 4.0 User Guide*.

Editing text

Adobe GoLive lets you edit text in your documents with the ease of using a word-processing application:

• You can delete text by selecting it and pressing Delete, choosing Edit > Cut, or pressing Ctrl+X (Windows) or Command+X (Mac OS).

• You can begin finding and correcting spelling errors by choosing Edit > Spellchecking.

• You can begin finding and replacing text by choosing Edit > Find.

Now you'll find the word "loud" and replace it with the word "powerful." You'll begin by setting preferences for finding text. You'll have Adobe GoLive keep the Find dialog box in front of the document window.

1 Choose Edit > Preferences.

2 In the Preferences dialog box, click the Find icon to display preferences for finding text.

3 Specify preferences:

• In Windows, choose Keep Find Window In Front from the menu, and click OK.

• In Mac OS, if the Hide Find Window If Match Is Found option is selected, deselect it. Then click OK.

Now you'll search for the text to replace.

4 Scroll up to bring the beginning of the document into view, and click before the main heading on the page to insert a cursor.

5 Choose Edit > Find.

6 In the Find dialog box, make sure that the Find & Replace tab is selected. Then type **loud** in the Find text box.

7 Click the arrow (▷) next to Replace to open the Replace text box. In the Replace text box, type **powerful**, and click Find.

The word "loud" is highlighted in the document.

8 In the Find dialog box, click Replace. In the document, "loud" is replaced with "powerful."

9 Close the Find dialog box, and choose File > Save.

You've completed the design of the Appraisal page for this lesson. Now you're ready to preview the page in Adobe GoLive.

Searching within a document and within a site

Using the Adobe GoLive search tools, you can find and replace text and HTML code elements in any file throughout your hard disk, simulate how Web search engines search your site, and you can search through complex sites for specific files.

Searching in the current document

You can use Find & Replace in Layout, Outline, or Source view. Depending on the view, you can search for text and some HTML code elements in the current document. Once you find what you're looking for, you can automatically change it to something else. You can also search for selected text without opening the Find dialog box.

–From the Adobe GoLive 4.0 User Guide, Chapter 4

Previewing the Web page in Adobe GoLive

1 In the document window, click the Preview tab.

Adobe GoLive displays a preview of the Appraisal page, and the Inspector changes to the Document Layout Controller.

2 In the Document Layout Controller, choose "Explorer 4 (Windows)" from the Root menu to see how your page appears in Internet Explorer 4 on a Windows platform. Try the different menu options and observe how your page changes in the preview. Notice that the text increases in size whenever you switch to a Windows-based browser.

3 Choose File > Close to close the Appraise.html file.

Previewing pages

The Adobe GoLive Preview mode lets you preview your work and test your links without launching an external application. When you preview a page using Preview, Adobe GoLive shows you "still photo" previews for plain pages and animated previews for QuickTime movies, animated GIFs, or any other of the plug-in media items supported. What you see closely resembles your page as finally published on the Web. You can also preview your pages using browsers. You need to preview in browsers, for example, to determine potential browser differences; you also need to use browsers to preview JavaScript, DHTML, Macromedia Shockwave™ animations, or other items Adobe GoLive doesn't provide native support for.

–From the Adobe GoLive 4.0 User Guide, Chapter 4

Exploring on your own

Hypertext Markup Language (HTML) is used to publish information on the World Wide Web. In this lesson, you worked in Adobe GoLive's Layout view to design a Web page. When you work in Layout view, Adobe GoLive writes HTML code for your page. Sometimes you may want to work directly with your page's HTML code. Adobe GoLive provides two different views of the HTML code, which you can use to design and edit your Web pages. Source view lets you view the HTML code directly, and Outline view lets you view the HTML code in a hierarchical, organized way.

Now that you've learned how to work in Layout view, try working in Source view and Outline view to make edits to the Appraisal page.

First you'll open the Appraisal page.

1 In Adobe GoLive, choose File > Open, and open the Appraise.html file, located inside the Lesson01/01End folder.

2 In the Appraise.html document window, select the main heading "Putting a Price on Your Guitar."

3 Click the Source tab to display the document in Source view.

4 Notice that the main heading is highlighted in the HTML source code. If necessary, use the scroll bars at the bottom of the document window and scroll to the right to bring the highlighted text into view.

Now you'll use the HTML Source Editor to change the paragraph format of the main heading from Header 1 to Header 2.

5 Select the text "h1" at the beginning of the line that contains the main heading. This text instructs the Web browser on how to display the main heading and is called a *tag*.

Selecting "h1" text

6 Type **h2** to replace the selected text.

7 Click the Layout tab to return the document to Layout view. Notice that the paragraph format for the main heading now is Header2.

Now you'll use the HTML Outline Editor to return the paragraph format of the main heading to Header 1.

8 Select the main heading.

9 Click the Outline tab to display the document in Outline view. Notice that the main heading has a black border around it in the outline.

10 Click to select the text "h2" located two lines above the main heading.

11 Type **h1** to replace the selected text, and click in the blank space outside the selected text to deselect it.

You'll also use the HTML Outline Editor to center the main heading on the page.

12 Click the arrow next to the "h1" text. A pop-up menu is displayed.

13 Choose "align" from the pop-up menu.

14 Click the arrow next to "align" to display another pop-up menu, and choose "center" from the pop-up menu.

Choosing "align" from pop-up menu

Choosing "center" from another pop-up menu

You'll also use the HTML Outline Editor to change the background color of the page to yellow.

15 In the Web 1 tab of the Color Palette, type **FFFFCC** in the Value text box, and press Enter. The selected color appears in the preview pane.

16 Drag the color from the preview pane to the color field for the background color of the page, located in line 9 of the outline.

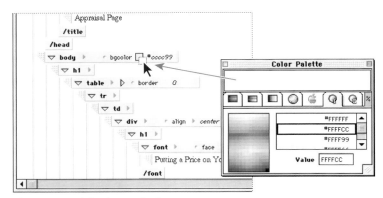

Changing page's background color

17 Click the Layout tab to return the document to Layout view. Notice that the paragraph format of the main heading now is Header 1, the main heading is centered on the page, and the background color of the page is yellow.

18 Choose File > Close to close the page. You don't need to save the changes you've made to it.

Review questions

1 Name two ways of adding text to a document.

2 How do you apply a paragraph style to text? How do you apply a physical style to text?

3 How do you change the color of text?

4 What's a common reason for putting all of the text in a document into a single-cell table?

5 Can you import data from a spreadsheet application into a table?

6 How do you add a caption to a table?

7 How do you learn more about the sets of fonts available for a document?

8 How can you begin finding and replacing text in a document?

Review answers

1 You can add text to a document by typing directly in the document window; importing text from another application into a table; using layout text boxes; using floating boxes; copying text from a document created in another application and pasting it into an Adobe GoLive document; and, dragging a text clip, created from a SimpleText or NotePad document, from the desktop to an Adobe GoLive document.

2 To apply a paragraph style, click anywhere in a paragraph, and choose a paragraph style from the Paragraph Format menu in the toolbar or the Format menu. To apply a physical style, select the text, and click the Bold, Italic, or Teletype button in the toolbar or choose a physical style from the Style menu.

3 To change the color of text, select the text, choose a color in the Color Palette, and drag the color from the preview pane of the Color Palette to the selected text on the page.

4 A common reason for putting all of the text in a document into a single-cell table is to control how text wraps on the page. Text in a single-cell table wraps at the set width of the table, even when the window size changes.

5 Yes, you can import data from most spreadsheet applications into a table. First, you need to export data from the spreadsheet application to a text-only file containing data separated by tabs. For more information, see the documentation for your spreadsheet application.

6 To add a caption to a table, select Caption in the Table Inspector, and choose Above Table or Below Table from the pop-up menu in the Table Inspector. Then click above or below the table to insert a cursor and type the text for the caption.

7 To learn more about the sets of fonts available for a document, choose Style > Font > Edit Font Sets to display the Font Set Editor. In the Font Set Editor, select a set of fonts to display its contents.

8 You can choose Edit > Find to begin finding and replacing text in a document.

Lesson 2

2 | Laying Out Web Pages

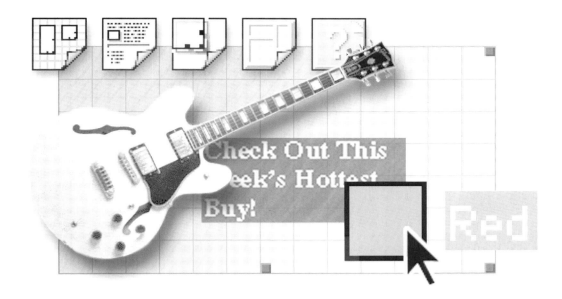

Adobe GoLive provides multiple ways for you to lay out your Web pages, so that you can precisely place text, images, and other objects on each page. It also provides several ways for you to save time when laying out your pages, so that you can quickly add objects and apply colors that are frequently used in your Web site. In this lesson, you'll explore the various tools for page layout as you work on the design of three pages.

In this lesson, you'll learn how to do the following:

• Create a new Web site, and add files to the site.

• Create a dynamic component that stores frequently used page content, and add the component to a page.

• Create a new page.

• Use a layout grid to place objects precisely on a page.

• Add images to a page using a variety of methods.

• Move, align, and distribute objects on a layout grid.

• Add a background image to a page.

• Add text to a page using layout text boxes.

• Create a custom color palette that stores frequently used colors, and add the colors to a page.

• Extract color from a region below the pointer.

• Use floating boxes to place overlapping objects on a page.

This lesson will take about an hour to complete.

If needed, remove the previous lesson folder from your hard drive and copy the Lesson02 folder onto it. As you work on this lesson, you'll overwrite the Start files. If you need to restore the Start files, copy them from the Adobe GoLive Classroom in a Book CD.

Getting started

In Lesson 1, "Working with Text," you designed a Web page for Gage Vintage Guitars. In this lesson, you'll create a Web site for the company and work on the design of three pages for the site.

First you'll view the finished Web pages in your browser.

1 Start your Web browser.

2 Open the Index.html file. In Windows, the path is Lesson02/02End/Gage Folder/Gage/Index.html. In Mac OS, the path is Lesson02/02End/ Gage *f* /Gage/Index.html.

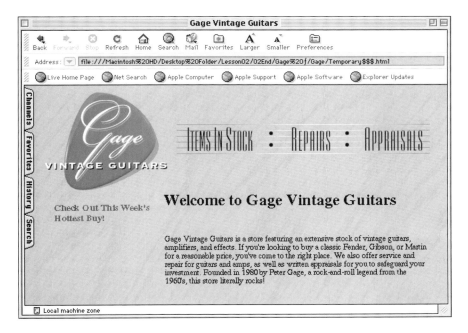

3 Open the Appraise.html file. In Windows, the path is Lesson02/02End/Gage Folder/Gage/Pages/Appraise.html. In Mac OS, the path is Lesson02/02End/ Gage *f* /Gage/Pages/Appraise.html.

4 Open the Hottest.html file. In Windows, the path is Lesson02/02End/Gage Folder/Gage/Pages/Hottest.html. In Mac OS, the path is Lesson02/02End/ Gage *f* /Gage/Pages/Hottest.html.

5 When you have finished viewing the pages, close them and quit your browser.

Creating a new Web site

You'll begin this lesson by creating a new Web site using Adobe GoLive.

1 Start Adobe GoLive. A new document named Untitled.html opens. You don't need a new document for this part of the lesson.

2 Choose File > Close to close Untitled.html.

Now you're ready to create a new Web site.

3 Choose File > New Site > Blank.

4 Type **Gage** as the name of the new site.

Note: If you are using Mac OS 8.1 and can't enter the name, press the Tab key three times and retype the name. You can also click Cancel to close the dialog box, choose Edit > Preferences > General > Display, deselect Use Navigation Services, click OK, and redo steps 3 and 4.

5 Select the Lesson02 folder. (In Windows, click Browse and use the pop-up dialog box to do this.)

6 Make sure that Create Folder is selected so that Adobe GoLive creates a folder for you.

7 In Windows, click OK. In Mac OS, click Save or Choose.

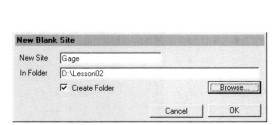

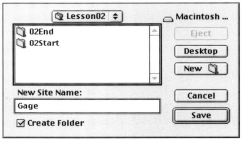

Creating new site (Windows)   *Creating new site (Mac OS)*

A folder named Gage Folder (Windows) or Gage *f* (Mac OS) is created within the Lesson02 folder. The site window appears with the Files tab selected and the Gage folder open.

8 Use Windows Explorer (Windows) or the Finder (Mac OS) to open the Gage Folder/Gage *f* folder, and examine its contents.

The Gage Folder/Gage *f* folder contains the following:

• The Gage folder, which stores the pages and media for your site. When you create a new site, this folder already contains a blank home page named Index.html.

• The Gage.data folder, which stores files for building and maintaining your site.

• The Gage.site (Windows) or Gage.π (Mac OS) file, which stores information about the structure of your site. When you open this file, the site window displays in Adobe GoLive.

Adding files to the Web site

Now you're ready to add files to the Web site. First you'll add a folder of image files. Later in this lesson, you'll use the image files when adding images to the pages for the site.

1 Using Windows Explorer (Windows) or the Finder (Mac OS), select the Images folder, located inside the Lesson02/02Start folder. Drag the Images folder from the desktop to the site window.

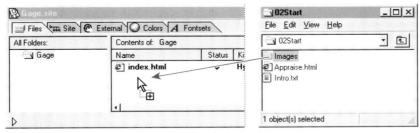

Dragging folder from desktop to site window (Windows)

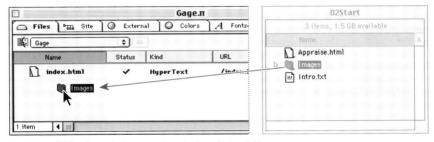

Dragging folder from desktop to site window (Mac OS)

2 In Mac OS, click the arrow (▷) next to the Images folder icon in the site window to display the contents of the Images folder.

Now you'll add a new folder to the site. This folder will store the pages for the site.

3 Choose Site > New > Group. A new untitled folder appears in the site window.

4 Type **Pages** to rename the folder, and click in the blank space outside the folder to deselect it.

Now you'll add the finished Web page from Lesson 1, "Working with Text," to the Pages folder. Later in this lesson, you'll update the design of the page.

5 Using Windows Explorer (Windows) or the Finder (Mac OS), select the Appraise.html file, located inside the Lesson02/02Start folder. Drag the Appraise.html file from the desktop to the Pages folder icon in the site window.

The Pages folder opens automatically in the site window, with Appraise.html inside it.

If you are using Adobe GoLive for Windows, go to the next section, "Creating a dynamic component," on page 83. If you are using Adobe GoLive for Mac OS, proceed with the following steps.

6 To return to the Gage folder, choose Gage from the menu in the upper left corner of the site window.

Returning to Gage folder

💡 *To move up one folder level in the site window, you can also click the Point & Shoot Navigation button (▲) in the site window.*

7 Click the arrow (▷) next to the Pages folder icon in the site window to display the folder's contents.

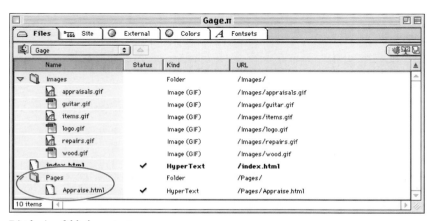

Displaying folder's contents

Creating a dynamic component

Now you're ready to begin designing the pages for the Web site. At the top of each page, you'll place the Gage Vintage Guitars logo and a navigation bar for the site. Instead of creating this page content multiple times, you'll create it once and save it as a *dynamic component* that you can quickly add to your pages.

Using dynamic components

Dynamic components let you create elements in one source file that you can use on multiple pages. This feature is useful for buttons, logos, headers, and other items that you want to use throughout your site.

About dynamic components

You can use Adobe GoLive components to reference other HTML pages and embed them in your page, complete with text, images, and other visual content. When you embed an element as a dynamic component instead of writing the HTML code in your pages, you can change the object simply by double-clicking it to open the source file (an HTML page containing only the element) and then editing the object. When you save the source page, Adobe GoLive automatically updates all pages that contain the element.

Adobe GoLive encloses the embedded HTML page in a custom tag that the browser ignores at run time (although its content is understood and interpreted correctly), and marks it as dynamic page content that needs to be updated each time the source file changes.

Note: *Dynamic components are updated only while you work on your local hard disk. Pages on the Web server are not updated by just uploading the source file. You need to upload all pages that reference a component to update your site after changing the source file.*

–From the Adobe GoLive 4.0 User Guide, Chapter 5

Now you'll create a new page that you'll save as a dynamic component.

1 Place the site window at the bottom of your desktop, so that the window is visible when you create a new page. To move a window, drag its title bar.

For detailed information about how to arrange your work area, see "Setting up your work area," on page 46.

2 Choose File > New to create a new page.

If needed, you can resize the document window and site window, so that they take up less space on the desktop. To resize a window, drag its lower right corner.

3 Select the page title, "Welcome to Adobe GoLive 4."

4 Type **Navigation Bar** as the new title, and click in the blank space beneath the title to deselect it.

5 Choose 580 from the Window Size menu in the lower right corner of the document window.

6 If necessary, choose View > Inspector (Windows) or Window > Inspector (Mac OS) to display the Inspector.

7 Click the Page icon (▤) in the upper left corner of the document window. The Inspector changes to the Page Inspector.

8 In the Page Inspector, click the HTML tab. Then click Component to set up the current page for use as a dynamic component.

9 Choose File > Save, rename the page **Navbar.html**, and save it in the Components folder. In Windows, the path is Lesson02/Gage Folder/Gage.data/Components. In Mac OS, the path is Lesson02/Gage ƒ /Gage.data/Components.

The Components folder stores dynamic components for the site. You can view the contents of this folder in the site window.

10 Display the expanded pane of the site window:

• In Windows, click the Aspect Control icon in the bottom left corner of the site window.

• In Mac OS, click the Aspect Control icon in the upper right corner of the site window.

The expanded pane of the site window is displayed, with the Extra tab selected and the Gage.data folder open. The contents of the Components folder are automatically displayed, because the folder contains a file.

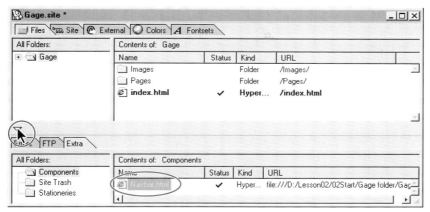

Components folder in expanded pane of site window (Windows)

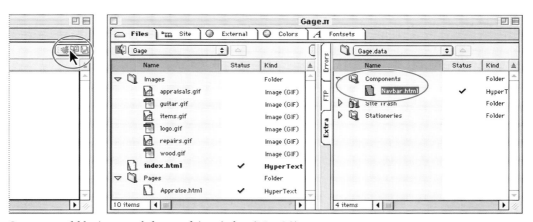

Components folder in expanded pane of site window (Mac OS)

Adding a layout grid

You can use a layout grid to place text, tables, images, and other objects precisely on a page. When you add a layout grid to a page, Adobe GoLive actually generates tables in the HTML source code for the page. It uses these tables to place the objects on the page with 1-pixel accuracy.

Now you'll add a layout grid to the page.

1 Click the Navbar.html window to make it active.

2 If necessary, choose View > Palette (Windows) or Window > Palette (Mac OS) to display the Palette, and make sure that the Basic tab (📄) is selected.

 3 Double-click the Layout Grid icon in the Palette, or drag the Layout Grid icon from the Palette to the page.

A layout grid is added to the page, and the Inspector changes to the Layout Grid Inspector.

Note: If the Inspector doesn't change to the Layout Grid Inspector, click the layout grid to select it, so that the Inspector changes accordingly. Throughout this book, if the Inspector doesn't change as stated in the instructions, select the appropriate object so that the Inspector changes accordingly.

Now you'll specify a width for the layout grid.

4 In the Layout Grid Inspector, type **580** for Width, and click the Enter button (↲) or press Enter or Return. (Whenever the Enter button appears after a text box, you must click the button or press Enter or Return on the keyboard to apply the value.)

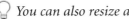 *You can also resize a layout grid by selecting it and dragging one of its handles.*

Adding an image using the Point and Shoot button

Now you'll add four images to the page using a variety of methods. Adobe GoLive supports the standard image formats for the Web: Graphical Interchange Format (GIF) and Joint Photographic Experts Group (JPEG). Typically, GIF images are used for line art and JPEG images are used for photographs and other images with more than 256 colors. In this lesson, you'll use GIF images.

First you'll add the company logo to the page using the Point and Shoot button in the Image Inspector.

 1 Drag the Image icon from the Palette to the upper left corner of the layout grid.

An image placeholder appears on the layout grid, and the Inspector changes to the Image Inspector.

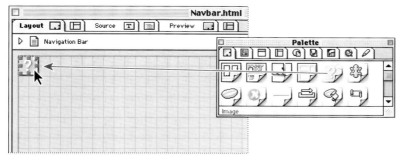

Adding image placeholder to page

2 In the Image Inspector, make sure that the Basic tab is selected.

Notice that the Source text box in the Image Inspector shows "Empty Reference!" This indicates that the image placeholder does not refer to an image yet. You'll use the Point and Shoot button to connect a specific image file in the site window with the image place-holder on the page.

3 Drag from the Point and Shoot button (⌖) in the Image Inspector to Logo.gif in the Images folder in the site window. Release the mouse button when Logo.gif is highlighted.

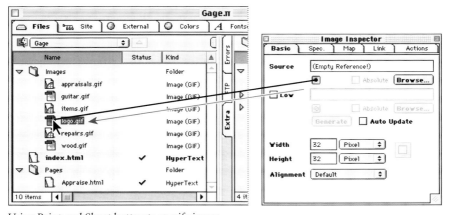

Using Point and Shoot button to specify image

The company logo is added to the page, and the Source text box in the Image Inspector shows the path to Logo.gif. If needed, you can easily adjust the position of the image by dragging it to the desired location.

Adobe GoLive supports the use of low-resolution images, which display in the viewer's browser while high-resolution images are loading. You can get low-resolution images from another source or generate them quickly using Adobe GoLive, as you'll do now.

4 Click Generate in the Image Inspector.

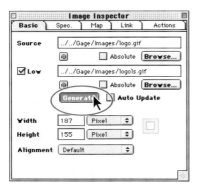

A low-resolution image named Logols.gif appears in the Images folder in the site window, and the Low option in the Image Inspector is automatically selected.

Now you'll add an alternative text message for the image. In browsers that don't support images or have image loading turned off, the text message is displayed instead of the image.

5 Click the Spec. (Special) tab in the Image Inspector. Type **Gage Vintage Guitars Logo** in the Alt Text box, and press Enter or Return.

6 Choose File > Save to save the page.

Adding an image using a keyboard shortcut

Now you'll add a second image to the page using a keyboard shortcut. This image is part of the navigation bar for the site.

1 Drag the Image icon from the Palette to the right of the company logo on the page.

2 Hold down Alt (Windows) or Command (Mac OS), and drag from the image place-holder on the page to Items.gif in the Images folder in the site window.

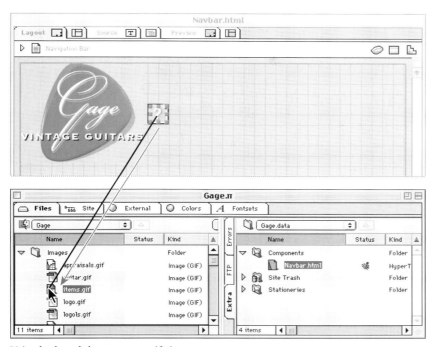

Using keyboard shortcut to specify image

3 In the Spec. tab of the Image Inspector, type **Items In Stock** in the Alt text box, and press Enter or Return to add an alternative text message for Items.gif.

Because Items.gif is small in file size (1K), you don't need to create a low-source image for it.

Adding images by dragging

You'll add the third and fourth images to the page by dragging. These images also are part of the navigation bar for the site.

Now you'll add the third image to the page.

1 Drag the Image icon from the Palette to the right of the Items In Stock image on the page.

2 Drag Repairs.gif from the Images folder in the site window to the image placeholder on the page.

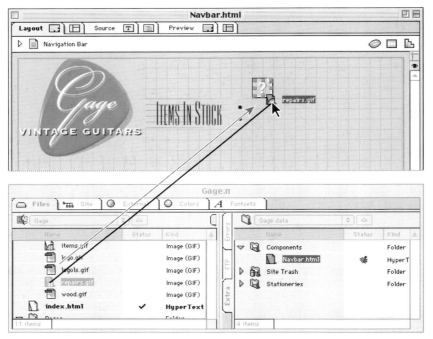

Dragging image file from site window to image placeholder

3 In the Image Inspector, type **Repairs** in the Alt text box, and press Enter or Return.

Now you'll add the fourth image to the page.

4 Drag the Image icon from the Palette to the right of the Repairs image on the page.

5 Drag Appraisals.gif from the Images folder in the site window to the image placeholder on the page.

6 In the Image Inspector, type **Appraisals** in the Alt text box, and press Enter or Return.

7 Choose File > Save to save the page.

💡 *To add an image, you can also drag the image file from the site window to the page, without using an image placeholder. Using an image placeholder gives you more control over the initial placement of the image.*

Aligning and distributing multiple objects

Now that you've added all of the images, you're ready to align and distribute them on the page. When you select more than one object on a layout grid, the Inspector changes to the Multiselection Inspector. While the toolbar lets you align objects relative to the layout grid, the Multiselection Inspector lets you both align and distribute objects relative to each other.

Now you'll align the tops of the three images that make up the navigation bar.

1 Click the Items In Stock image to select it. Then Shift-click the Repairs image and the Appraisals image to add them to the selection.

The Inspector changes to the Multiselection Inspector.

2 In the Multiselection Inspector, make sure that the Alignment tab is selected. Click the Align Top button ( ) to align the tops of the selected objects. (The button is dimmed if the tops of the selected objects are already aligned.)

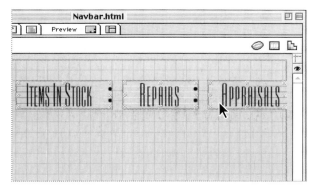

Shift-clicking to select multiple objects   *Align Top button*

Now you'll distribute the images horizontally. You'll specify an offset of 0 to remove any space between the images.

3 Click the Special tab in the Multiselection Inspector.

4 Under Horizontal, make sure that Offset is selected. Type **0** in the Offset text box, and press Enter or Return. Then click the Equidistant Edges button ( ).

The selected objects are moved horizontally on the page so that their edges are equally spaced by 0 pixels, the value specified in the Offset text box.

You can move a selected object on a layout grid using the arrow keys. By default, pressing an arrow key moves the object 16 pixels, the spacing between the horizontal and vertical lines of the grid.

5 With the three images still selected, use the Up arrow key to move the images to the top of the layout grid. Then use the Left arrow key to move the images next to the company logo.

If a layout grid has options selected to snap objects to the grid, you can easily move a selected object on the grid by 1 pixel. Hold down Ctrl+Alt (Windows) or Option (Mac OS), and press an arrow key.

6 Click in the blank space beneath the selected images to deselect them.

You may have noticed that the layout grid increased in size as necessary to accommodate the images that you added to it. When you've finished placing objects on a layout grid, it's a good idea to optimize the grid. Optimizing a grid reduces its size, so that it takes up less space on the page.

Now you'll optimize the layout grid.

7 If necessary, click the layout grid to select it. Then click Optimize in the Layout Grid Inspector.

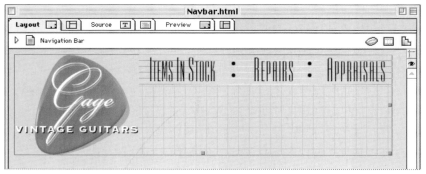

Optimized layout grid

8 Choose File > Save to save the page. Then choose File > Close to close it.

Designing the home page

Now you're ready to design the home page for the Web site.

1 In the site window, double-click Index.html to open it. (In Windows, double-click the Gage folder icon in the site window to display Index.html.)

2 Change the title of the page to **Gage Vintage Guitars**.

3 Choose 580 from the Window Size menu in the lower right corner of the document window.

Adding a background image

Now you'll add a background image to the home page. When choosing a background image, you can choose an image that's smaller in size than your page. Adobe GoLive, as well as Web browsers, treats the background image as a tile that it repeats to cover the page.

First you'll preview the image. You can use the File Inspector to obtain detailed information about a file, including a preview of its contents.

1 In the site window, click the icon for Wood.gif in the Images folder. (Be sure to click the icon, not the filename.) The Inspector changes to the File Inspector.

2 Click the Content tab in the File Inspector. A preview of Wood.gif appears in the File Inspector.

Now you'll add a background image to the page using Wood.gif.

3 Click the Page icon (▤) in the upper left corner of the document window. The Inspector changes to the Page Inspector.

4 In the Page Inspector, click the Page tab. Click the check box next to Image to select the Image option.

5 Drag from the Point and Shoot button (⬚) in the Page Inspector to Wood.gif in the Images folder in the site window.

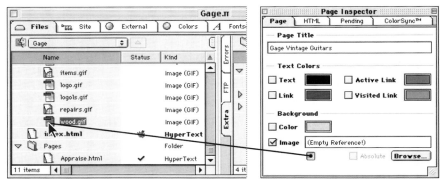

Specifying image to tile for page's background

The image of the wood is tiled to cover the page.

Adding a dynamic component

Now you'll add the navigation bar to the home page using the dynamic component that you created earlier in this lesson.

 1 Click the CyberObjects tab (⬚) in the Palette. Then drag the Component icon to the upper left corner of the page.

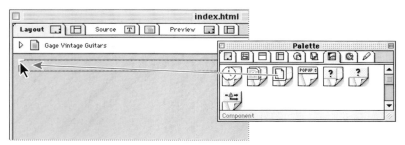

Adding component placeholder to page

The Inspector changes to the Component Inspector.

2 Drag from the Point and Shoot button (📷) in the Component Inspector to Navbar.html in the Components folder in the site window. (Remember that the Components folder is displayed in the expanded pane of the site window.)

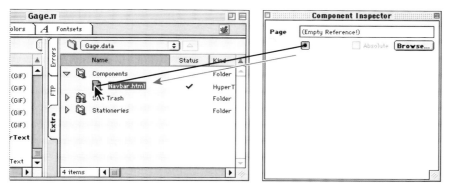

Using Point and Shoot button to specify component

The navigation bar is added to the top of the home page.

3 Choose File > Save to save the page.

Adding text using layout text boxes

Now you'll add text to the page using layout text boxes. Before you can add layout text boxes to the page, you must add a layout grid to the page. You place the layout text boxes on the grid and then type text in the boxes. With layout text boxes, you can easily rearrange the location of text on your page by moving or aligning the boxes.

First you'll add a layout grid to the home page.

 1 Click the Basic tab (▣) in the Palette. Then double-click the Layout Grid icon in the Palette, or drag the Layout Grid icon from the Palette to below the component on the page.

2 Type **580** for Width in the Layout Grid Inspector, and press Enter or Return.

Now you're ready to add the first layout text box to the page. You'll use this box to add a main heading to the page.

 3 Drag the Layout Text Box icon from the Palette to the upper center of the new layout grid.

A layout text box is added to the page. If needed, you can easily adjust the position of the box. Move the pointer to an edge of the box, so that the pointer turns into a hand. Then drag the box to the desired location.

4 Click inside the layout text box, and type **Welcome to Gage Vintage Guitars**. Then choose Header 1 from the Paragraph Format menu in the toolbar.

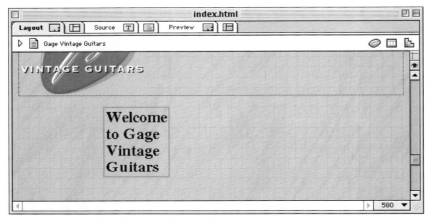

Text in layout text box, reformatted as Header 1

You can use the toolbar to position a selected object precisely on a layout grid.

5 Click an edge of the layout text box to select it.

6 In the toolbar, type **180** in the Horizontal Position text box, and press Enter or Return to position the box 180 pixels from the left edge of the grid. Type **0** in the Vertical Position text box, and press Enter or Return to position the box 0 pixels from the top of the grid.

You can also use the toolbar to resize a selected object.

7 In the toolbar, type **400** in the X size text box, and press Enter or Return to make the box 400 pixels in width. Type **80** in the Y size text box, and press Enter or Return to make the box 80 pixels in height.

Now you'll add a second layout text box to the page. You'll use this box to add a subheading to the page.

8 Drag the Layout Text Box icon from the Palette to the upper left of the layout grid.

9 Click inside the layout text box, and type: **Check Out This Week's Hottest Buy!** Then select the text you've just typed, click the Bold button (**B**) in the toolbar, and choose 4 from the Font Size menu in the toolbar.

If needed, you can resize the layout text box using its handles. Click an edge of the box to select it, and drag one of its handles.

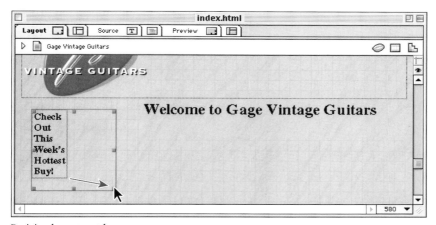

Resizing layout text box

10 Click in the blank space outside the layout text box to deselect it.

Adding text using a table

Now you'll add text to the page that introduces Gage Vintage Guitars. You'll begin by creating a single-cell table. Then you'll import text into the table from a text-only file created in a word-processing application.

For more information about working with tables, see "Adding tables," on page 56.

1 Drag the Table icon from the Palette to below the main heading on the layout grid.

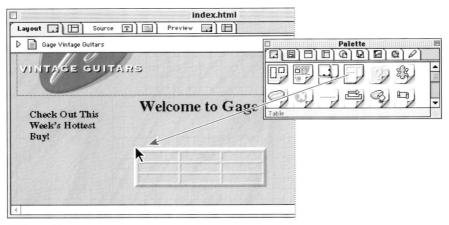

Adding table to page

The Inspector changes to the Table Inspector, with the Table tab selected.

2 In the Table Inspector, type **1** for Rows, and press Enter or Return. Type **1** for Columns, and press Enter or Return.

3 Choose Pixel from the menu to the right of the Width text box. For Width, type **400**, and press Enter or Return.

4 Type **0** for Border, and press Enter or Return to remove the table's border.

5 Click the Browse button for the Import Tab-Text option.

6 Select the Intro.txt file, located inside the Lesson02/02Start folder, and click Open.

7 In the toolbar, type **180** in the Horizontal Position text box, and press Enter or Return. Type **80** in the Vertical Position text box, and press Enter or Return.

8 Choose File > Save to save the page.

Creating a custom color palette and adding color to text

Now you'll add color to some of the text on the page. You'll begin by adding a color to the Colors tab in the site window. You can use the Colors tab as a custom color palette to store colors that you frequently use in your site.

1 Click the Colors tab in the site window.

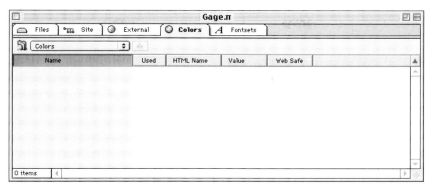

Colors tab in site window

2 If necessary, choose View > Color Palette (Windows) or Window > Color Palette (Mac OS) to display the Color Palette.

3 In the Color Palette, make sure that the Web I tab ( ) is selected. In the Value text box, type **990000**, and press Enter or Return. The selected color appears in the preview pane.

4 Drag the color from the preview pane to the site window.

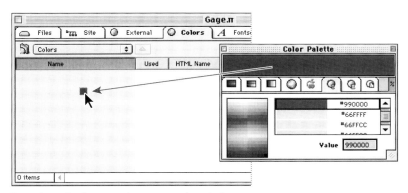

Dragging color from preview pane to site window

5 Type **Red** as the name of the color, and press Enter or Return. Then click in the blank space beneath the color name to deselect it.

Now you'll color some of the text on the page using the Red color.

6 Select the text: "Check Out This Week's Hottest Buy!" (Make sure that you select the text, not the text box.)

7 Drag the Red color from the site window to the selected text on the page.

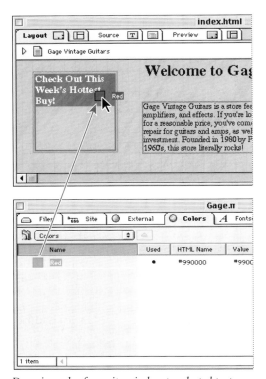

Dragging color from site window to selected text

8 Click in the blank space outside the selected text to deselect it.

You can also extract color from a region below the pointer and add the color to your custom color palette. This feature is useful when you want to match the colors of two objects.

9 Move the pointer over the checkerboard colors field in the Color Palette, so that it turns into an eyedropper.

10 Drag from the checkerboard colors field to the shadow of the guitar pick on the page, and release the mouse button. The color of the shadow appears in the preview pane of the Color Palette.

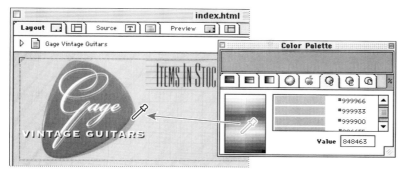

Extracting color from image on page

11 Drag the new color from the preview pane to the site window.

12 Type **Olive** as the name of the color, and press Enter or Return. Then click in the blank space beneath the color name to deselect it.

If desired, you can now match objects on the page with the color of the shadow. The site window provides information about whether or not a color is Web safe. In the Web Safe column of the site window, the Olive color does not have a bullet, indicating that the color will dither on a system set to 256 display colors (standard PCs).

13 Select the layout grid below the navigation bar, and click Optimize in the Layout Grid Inspector.

14 Choose File > Save to save the home page. Then choose File > Close to close it.

Now you're ready to design two other pages for the Gage Vintage Guitars Web site.

Updating the design of the Appraisal page

First you'll update the design of the finished Web page from Lesson 1, "Working with Text."

Adding a dynamic component

Currently, the page does not contain the navigation bar for the site. You'll add the navigation bar quickly using the dynamic component you created earlier in this lesson.

1 Click the Files tab in the site window.

2 In the site window, double-click Appraise.html in the Pages folder to open it.

3 Choose 580 from the Window Size menu in the lower right corner of the document window.

Earlier in this lesson, you learned how to add a dynamic component by first adding a Component placeholder to the page. Now you'll learn how to add a dynamic component without using a placeholder.

4 Click the Site Extras tab (⊡) in the Palette.

5 Choose Components from the menu in the lower right corner of the Palette. An icon of the dynamic component, Navbar.html, appears in the Palette.

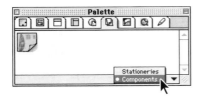

6 Drag the icon of Navbar.html in the Palette to the upper left corner of the page.

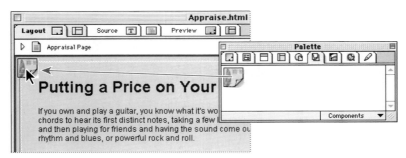

Using icon in Palette to add dynamic component

7 If necessary, scroll up to bring the beginning of the document into view.

The navigation bar is added to the top of the Appraisal page. Notice that the Page text box in the Component Inspector shows the path to Navbar.html.

Updating a custom color palette

Now you'll update your custom color palette with any colors from the Appraisal page that aren't already in the palette.

1 Click the Colors tab in the site window, and then click the Update button (✔) in the toolbar.

A folder named New Colors is added to the site window. It contains new colors from the page: the background color of the page and the colors of the table cells.

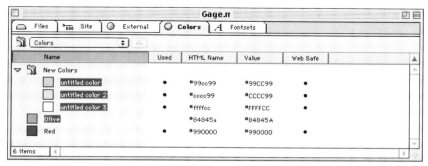

Updated custom color palette

You'll name each of the colors.

2 Click in the blank space outside the selected colors to deselect them.

3 Click the name of the first untitled color to select it. (Be sure to click the name, not the icon.) Type **Green**, and press Enter or Return. Then click in the blank space beneath the name to deselect it.

4 Change the name of the second untitled color to **Khaki**, and change the name of the third untitled color to **Yellow**.

Now you'll change the name of the New Colors folder, and move the Olive and Red colors inside the folder.

5 Click the name of the New Colors folder to select it. Type **Gage Colors**, and press Enter or Return.

6 In Windows, double-click the Colors folder icon to display the contents of the Color folder.

7 Click the icon for the Olive color to select it, and Shift-click the icon for the Red color to add it to the selection. Then drag the selected colors to the Gage Colors folder.

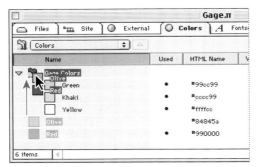
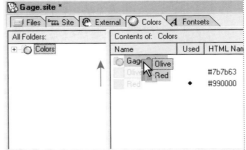

Dragging colors inside folder (Mac OS)   *Dragging colors inside folder (Windows)*

8 In Windows, double-click the Gage Colors folder icon to display the contents of the Gage Colors folder.

9 Click the title bar of the Appraisal page to activate it. Choose File > Save to save the page. Then choose File > Close to close it.

Designing the Hottest Buy page

Now you'll design a new page using floating boxes. Floating boxes let you place objects on the page intuitively, without using of a table or layout grid. They also let you overlap objects on a page in layers. You can add text, tables, images, and other objects to floating boxes.

First you'll create a new page.

1 Choose File > New.

2 Change the title of the page to **Hottest Buy**.

3 Choose 580 from the Window Size menu in the lower right corner of the document window.

4 Choose File > Save, rename the page **Hottest.html**, and save it in the Pages folder. In Windows, the path is Lesson02/Gage Folder/Gage/Pages. In Mac OS, the path is Lesson02/Gage ƒ /Gage/Pages.

Now you'll change the background color of the page. Using your custom color palette, you can easily match the background color of the page with the background color of the Appraisal page.

5 Drag the Khaki color from the site window to the Page icon (![page icon]) in the upper left corner of the document window.

The background color of the page changes to khaki.

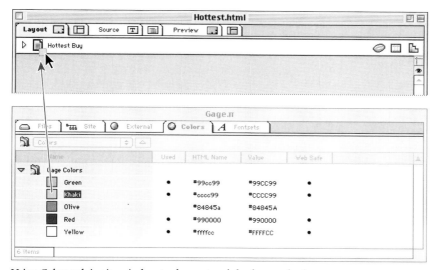

Using Colors tab in site window to change page's background color

Now you'll add the navigation bar to the page, as you did with the other pages for the site.

6 Drag the icon of Navbar.html in the Site Extras tab of the Palette to the upper left corner of the page.

7 Choose File > Save to save the page.

Adding the first floating box

Now you'll add a floating box to the page. You'll use this floating box to add an image of a guitar to the page.

1 Click the Basic tab in the Palette. Then double-click the Floating Box icon in the Palette, or drag the Floating Box icon from the Palette to the page.

A floating box appears on the page in the upper left corner below the component, and the Inspector changes to the Floating Box Inspector.

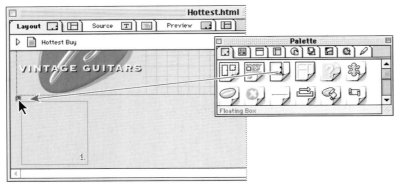

Adding floating box to page

Now you'll name the floating box, so that you can differentiate it from other floating boxes that you'll add to the page.

2 In the Floating Box Inspector, type **Image** in the Name text box, and press Enter or Return.

Now you'll add the guitar image to the floating box.

3 Click the Files tab in the site window. Then drag Guitar.gif from the Images folder in the site window to the floating box on the page.

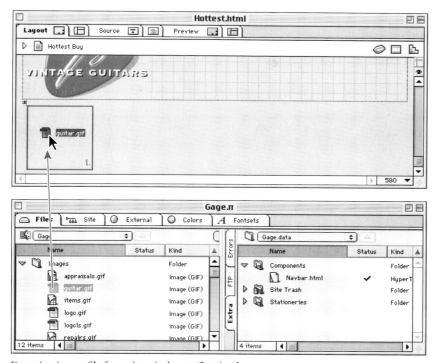

Dragging image file from site window to floating box

The guitar image appears in the floating box.

4 Click in the blank space outside the image to deselect it.

Adding the second floating box

You'll add a second floating box to the page that will contain a description of the guitar you've just added to the page.

1 Double-click the Floating Box icon in the Palette. The second floating box appears on top of the first one.

2 In the Floating Box Inspector, type **Description** in the Name text box, and press Enter or Return.

For now, you'll move the Description floating box to an empty area of the page.

3 Move the pointer over an edge of the Description floating box, so that the pointer turns into a hand pointing left. (If the hand is pointing up, an object other than the floating box is selected.)

4 Drag the Description floating box to the right of the Image floating box.

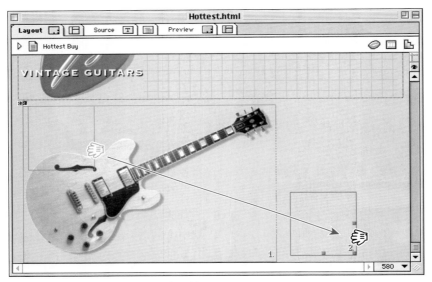

Dragging second floating box to right of first one

Now you'll add text to the Description floating box. You'll enter a description of the guitar shown on the page.

5 Click inside the Description floating box, and type **1981 Gibson ES-347**. Then select the text you've just typed, click the Bold button (**B**) in the toolbar, and choose 6 from the Font Size menu in the toolbar.

6 Click the Colors tab in the site window. Then drag the Red color from the site window to the selected text on the page.

7 Click in the blank space outside the selected text to deselect it.

💡 *You can also display custom colors for your site in the Site Colors tab of the Color Palette. Then you can use the Color Palette instead of the site window to apply color to the page.*

Now you'll move the Description floating box using the Floating Box Inspector.

8 Move the pointer over an edge of the Description floating box, so that the pointer turns into a hand pointed to the left. Then click an edge of the floating box to select it.

9 In the Floating Box Inspector, type **250** for Left, and press Enter or Return to position the floating box 250 pixels from the left edge of the page. Type **300** for Top, and press Enter or Return to position the floating box 300 pixels from the top of the page.

Now you'll resize the floating box using the Floating Box Inspector.

10 Type **200** for Width, and press Enter or Return to make the floating box 200 pixels in width. Type **100** for Height, and press Enter or Return to make the floating box 100 pixels in height.

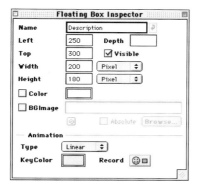

You can also resize a floating box by selecting it and dragging one of its handles.

11 Choose File > Save to save the page.

Notice that the Items In Stock, Repairs, and Appraisals images on the Hottest Buy page are aligned to the top of the grid. You'll move these images down so that they're vertically centered on the grid.

12 Try to click an image to select it for editing. Notice that you selected the entire dynamic component instead.

You can't edit the objects in the dynamic component from this page. Instead, you edit the objects in the component from the file in which you created them.

13 Choose File > Close to close the page.

Using floating boxes

Floating boxes let you manipulate page content to create dynamic effects and multilayered displays. Floating boxes let you divide your page into rectangles that you can format individually, fill with HTML content, and stack. The boxes can be opaque or transparent to reveal objects in the background.

Note: *To display properly, floating boxes require Web browsers version 4.0 or later. Although floating boxes may soon be used as commonly as HTML tables, viewers with older browsers may have trouble viewing pages that contain floating boxes.*

About floating boxes

Floating boxes are based on the DIV tag, which has been available since HTML 3.2 but not commonly used. HTML 4.0 substantially enhances the DIV tag's functionality, allowing it to be absolutely positioned, and stacked to accept a background image or background color. The DIV tag is also a core element of Dynamic HTML and a major building block for absolute positioning with cascading style sheets.

Two concepts are key to understanding floating boxes:

• Layering is a key feature of floating boxes. Floating boxes can overlap or even be placed on top of each other. The stacking order is controlled by an attribute called the z-index (z is from the z-axis in a three-dimensional coordinate system). Elements with a higher z-index display on top of elements with a lower z-index. For example, an element with a z-index of 2 appears to float above an element with a z-index of 1. By default, floating boxes are superimposed on the normal flow of HTML and the Adobe GoLive layout grid.

• As an independent division within the page, a floating box accepts any other HTML tag—such as an image or simple HTML text with formatting. It also has the same background image and color properties as an HTML page.

–From the Adobe GoLive 4.0 User Guide, Chapter 5

Editing a dynamic component

An additional benefit of using a dynamic component to place frequently used page content throughout your site is that you only need to edit a single file to make changes to the component. When you save your changes to the component, Adobe GoLive automatically updates all files that use it.

Now you'll open Navbar.html to edit it.

1 Click the Files tab in the site window.

2 In the Components folder in the site window, double-click Navbar.html to open it.

3 Click the Items In Stock image to select it. Then Shift-click the Repairs image and the Appraisals image to add them to the selection.

4 Click the Vertical Align Center button ( ) in the toolbar to center the images vertically on the grid.

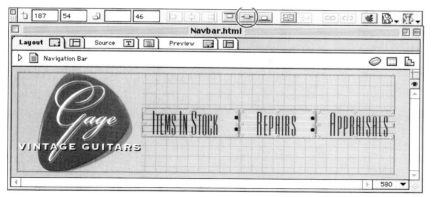

Images centered vertically on grid

5 Click in the blank space outside the selected images to deselect them.

6 Choose File > Save to save the page. Click OK for Adobe GoLive to automatically update the files that use Navbar.html as a dynamic component.

7 Choose File > Close to close the page.

You've completed the design of the Web site for this lesson. Now you're ready to preview the pages in Adobe GoLive.

Previewing the Web pages in Adobe GoLive

To preview each Web page, do the following:

1 In the site window, double-click Index.html, Appraise.html, or Hottest.html to open it. (The Appraise.html and Hottest.html files are located inside the Pages folder.)

2 In the document window, click the Preview tab.

Adobe GoLive displays a preview of the page, and the Inspector changes to the Document Layout Controller. Notice that the location of the navigation bar has moved down on the page to reflect the change you made to the dynamic component.

3 In the Document Layout Controller, choose "Explorer 4 (Windows)" from the Root menu to see how your page appears in Internet Explorer 4 on the Windows platform. Try the different menu options and observe how your page changes in the preview.

4 When you have finished viewing the page, choose File > Close to close it.

5 When you have finished viewing all of the pages, choose File > Close to close the site window.

Exploring on your own

Sometimes you may want several pages in your Web site to be similar in page layout and design. Instead of creating each page from scratch, you can create the page once and save it as stationery. In Adobe GoLive, stationery is equivalent to page templates available in most word-processing applications. You save a page as stationery and use the stationery to create new pages that are fully editable.

Try creating stationery from the home page for the Gage Vintage Guitars site. Then use the stationery to create a new page.

1 Choose File > Open, and open the Gage.site (Windows) or Gage.π (Mac OS) file. In Windows, the path is Lesson02/02End/Gage Folder/Gage.site. In Mac OS, the path is Lesson02/02End/Gage ƒ /Gage.π.

2 In the site window, double-click Index.html to open it.

3 Choose File > Save As, rename the page **Master.html**, and save it in the Stationeries folder. In Windows, the path is Lesson02/02End/Gage Folder/Gage.data/Stationeries. In Mac OS, the path is Lesson02/02End/Gage ƒ /Gage.data/Stationeries.

4 Choose File > Close to close the page.

5 Click the Site Extras tab (▣) in the Palette.

6 Choose Stationeries from the menu in the lower right corner of the Palette. An icon of the stationery, Master.html, appears in the Palette.

7 Drag the icon of Master.html in the Palette to the Pages folder in the site window. A new page from the Master.html stationery appears in the site window.

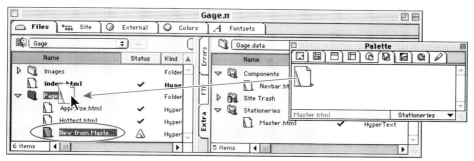

Creating new page from stationery

8 Type **New.html** to rename the page, and press Enter or Return. Then click in the blank space outside the filename to deselect it.

9 In the site window, double-click New.html in the Pages folder to open it.

10 Click the navigation bar at the top of the page. Notice that you selected the entire dynamic component. As with other pages that use the dynamic component, you can't edit the objects in the component from this page. Instead, you edit the objects in the component from the file in which you created them.

11 Select the text: "Check Out This Week's Hottest Buy!"

12 Type new text as desired to replace the selected text. (We used: "Click Here for a Free Appraisal!") Notice that you can edit the text in the layout text boxes on the page.

You can also remove objects from the page.

13 Click the left edge of the single-cell table to select it. (The table contains the text that introduces Gage Vintage Guitars.) Press Delete to remove the table.

You can also add objects to the page.

14 Click the Basic tab (⬚) in the Palette, and drag the Layout Text Box icon from the Palette to the layout grid on the page. A layout text box is added to the page.

15 If desired, continue to make changes to the page. When you have finished, choose File > Close to close the page. You don't need to save your changes. Then choose File > Close to close the site window.

Review questions

1 Which file displays in the site window?

2 Name two benefits of using a dynamic component.

3 How can you add a dynamic component to a page?

4 What are the two standard image formats for the Web?

5 Name two ways that you can specify an image for an image placeholder on a page.

6 What object needs to be present before adding a layout text box to a page?

7 How do you create a custom color palette?

8 Can you extract color from an image that you've added to a page? If so, how?

9 Why do you name floating boxes?

10 How do you move a floating box?

Review answers

1 In Windows, the file with the .site extension displays in the site window. In Mac OS, the file with the .π extension displays in the site window.

2 Using a dynamic component, you can create repetitive page content once and then quickly add it to the pages for your site. You can also make edits to repetitive page content in a single file and then have Adobe GoLive automatically update pages in your site that use the component.

3 You can add a dynamic component to a page by doing one of the following:

• Drag the Component icon from the CyberObjects tab in the Palette to the page. Then drag from the Point and Shoot button in the Component Inspector to an HTML file in the Components folder in the site window.

• Choose Components from the menu in the lower right corner of the Site Extras tab in the Palette. Then drag the icon of the HTML file from the Palette to the page.

4 The two standard image formats for the Web are Graphical Interchange Format (GIF) and Joint Photographic Experts Group (JPEG).

5 You can specify an image for an image placeholder by doing one of the following: drag from the Point and Shoot button in the Image Inspector to an image file in the site window; hold down Alt (Windows) or Command (Mac OS), and drag from the image placeholder to an image file in the site window; or, drag an image file from the site window to the image placeholder.

6 A layout grid needs to be present before adding a layout text box to a page.

7 Using the Color Palette, choose a color that you want in your custom color palette. Then drag the color from the preview pane of the Color Palette to the Colors tab in the site window. When the Colors tab in the site window is selected, you can also quickly create a custom color palette by opening a new page that has color applied and clicking the Update button in the toolbar.

8 Yes, you can extract color from an image that you've added to a page. Drag from the checkerboard colors field to a specific area of the image on the page, and release the mouse button. The color of the area of the image appears in the preview pane of the Color Palette.

9 You name floating boxes so that you can differentiate them from one another.

10 Move the pointer over an edge of the floating box, so that the pointer turns into a hand pointed to the left. Drag the floating box to move it.

Lesson 3

3 | Links

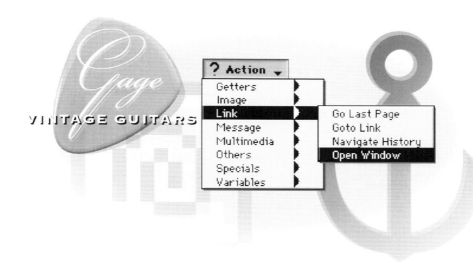

Once you've created content for your Web pages, you must give viewers a way to get from one page to another. Hyperlinks let site visitors jump from one page location—text or graphics—to another.

In this lesson, you'll learn how to do the following:

• Add links to graphics on a page.

• Add an anchor to the page that acts as a bookmark for information later on the page.

• Add hypertext links to a page.

• Add an action to a link spot.

• Change a link's color and highlight.

• Verify links.

• Create clickable image maps and link them to a Web page.

• Add hot spots to an image map and change their shape.

• Edit links and anchors.

• Fix broken links and change link preferences.

This lesson will take about 45 minutes to complete. If needed, remove the previous lesson folder from your hard drive and copy the Lesson03 folder onto it. As you work on this lesson, you'll overwrite the Start files. If you need to restore the Start files, copy them from the Adobe GoLive Classroom in a Book CD.

For information on setting up your work area, see "Setting up your work area" on page 46.

About links

Links allow users to jump to related information (text or image) using hyperlinks:

• Locally within a site.

• To locations on the same page as the link (called anchors).

• Across the Web.

• To non-Web resources such as FTP servers, newsgroups, and e-mail addresses.

The lesson folder contains a product page for a vintage guitar site, with companion pages for guitar equipment, special offers, appraisal information, and repair sites.

Getting started

In this lesson, you'll explore linking from graphics and text, called hypertext links; creating image maps; and, adding an action to a link. You'll start the lesson by viewing the final lesson file in your browser, to see what you'll accomplish.

1 Start your browser.

2 Choose File > Open and open the Index.html file:

• In Windows, the path is Lesson03/03End/Gage Folder/Gage folder/Index.html.

• In Mac OS, the path is Lesson03/03End/Gage ƒ /Gage folder/Index.html.

Final Index.html file, previewed in Netscape browser

3 Click the links in the Index.html file, and explore the site.

4 When you have finished viewing the file, close it. Close your browser.

Opening a site

Follow these steps to open the site and begin this lesson's work.

1 Start Adobe GoLive.

2 Close the empty document that appears in the document window in Layout view.

3 Choose File > Open, and open the Gage.site (Windows) or Gage.π (Mac OS) file:

• In Windows, the path is Lesson03/ 03Start/Gage Folder/Gage.

• In Mac OS, the path is Lesson 03/03Start/ Gage ƒ /Gage.π.

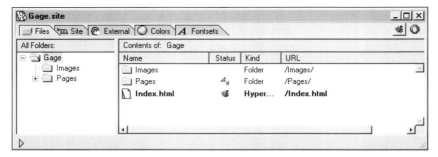

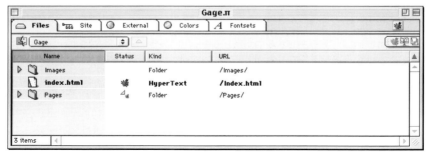

Windows Gage site window (top); Mac OS Gage site window (bottom)

This site consists of the Index.html file, the Images folder, which contains images for the site, and the Pages folder, which contains separate HTML pages that you'll link.

4 In the site window, double-click the Index.html file to open it. This is the home page for the vintage guitar site.

As you work on this lesson, you'll overwrite the Start files. If you need to restore the Start files, copy them from the Adobe GoLive Classroom in a Book CD.

Creating a link from a graphic

Adding links to a page lets viewers jump to other pages in the site. Now you'll create a link from the Index.html file to the Stock page, so that viewers can jump from the home page to a list of items in stock for the site.

You'll start by seeing whether the file contains any links, and determining where and how to add a link to the Index.html file.

1 Click the Preview tab (▭) at the top of the Index.html file document window, so that you can work for a moment in Preview view.

2 Using the pointer, click various places in the document window. Notice that the file has no links.

3 Click the Layout tab (▭) of the Index.html file to return to Layout view.

4 In the document window of the Index.html file, click the Items in Stock image to try to select it. You won't be able to select the image because it's actually part of a dynamic component—an element that updates automatically across a site when you change the element.

Selecting an unlinked graphic within a dynamic component

To create the link, you must open the dynamic component and add it to that file. You'll do that in the next steps.

Dynamic components let you easily manage repetitive content, such as headers, footers, and other recurring design elements, by storing them in a single file instead of inserting them physically wherever they occur. (For instructions on creating a component, see "Creating a dynamic component" on page 83.)

You'll add the link to the component so that any changes you make later to the link will be applied automatically across the site. Adding a link to a dynamic component uses the same technique as creating any hyperlink.

5 Open the Navbar.html file using any of these techniques:

• Double-click the Navbar component in the document window.

• Choose File > Open and open the file. In Windows, the path is Lesson03/03Start/ Gage Folder/Gage.data folder/components/Navbar.html. In Mac OS, the path is Lesson03/03Start/Gage ƒ /Gage.data folder/components/Navbar.html.

• In Windows, click the icon at the bottom left of the site window to display all of the site contents. At the top of the split site window, click the Extra tab to display the site's Gage.data folder and its contents. (You may have to drag the site window up to display all of its contents.) Double-click the Components folder to open it; then double-click the Navbar.html file to open it.

• In Mac OS, click the icon (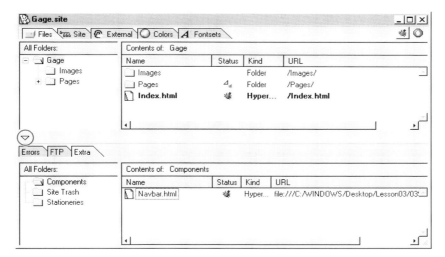) in the top right corner of the title bar of the site window to display all of the site contents. On the left side of the split screen, click the Extra tab to display the site's Gage.data folder and its contents. Double-click the Components folder to open it; then double-click the Navbar.html file to open it.

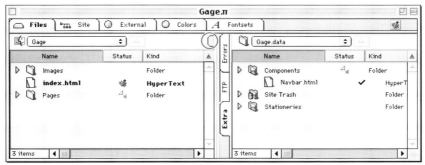

Windows expanded site window (top); Mac OS expanded site window (bottom)

When a dynamic component is embedded in your pages, you can easily edit the component by editing the source file (in this case, the HTML page containing only the header) and then letting Adobe GoLive automatically update all pages.

6 If it isn't open, choose View > Inspector (Windows) or Window > Inspector (Mac OS) to display the Inspector.

7 In the document window, click the Items in Stock graphic to select it. The Image Inspector becomes active.

8 Click the Link tab in the Image Inspector. You use this palette to specify links.

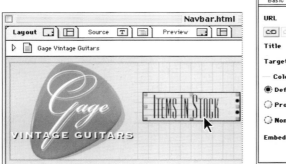

Selecting a graphic within a dynamic component   *Link tab of Image Inspector*

You can also create a new link by clicking the New Link button in the toolbar, as you'll do later in this lesson.

You'll create your first link by using the Point and Shoot button in the Image Inspector to link to a file in the site window. You can create links using various techniques. The easiest, most intuitive approach to creating a link is the point and shoot method.

9 If necessary, arrange the document window, site window, and Image Inspector so that all three are visible on your desktop.

10 In the Link tab in the Image Inspector, click the New Link button (⌘). Then position the pointer on the Point and Shoot button.

11 Drag from the Point and Shoot button (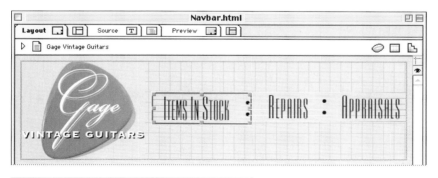) to the Stock.html file inside the Pages folder in the site window. If the Stock.html file isn't visible, position the pointer over the icon to the left of the Pages folder until the folder opens; then drag to select the file.

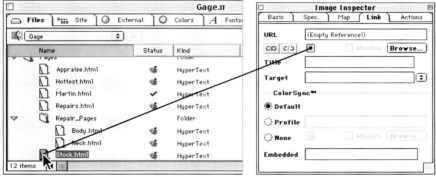

Using Point and Shoot button to link from Items in Stock image to Stock.html file

12 Release the mouse button when the interconnecting line blinks twice and the filename and directory path appear in the URL text box in the Text Inspector. (If the link can't be made, the line snaps back to the Point and Shoot button.)

The file's URL appears in the URL text box in the Image Inspector. You've created your first link.

A border appears around the image to indicate that it's now a link. You'll get rid of the border.

13 Click the Spec. (Special) tab in the Image Inspector. Select the Border option and enter **0**. In the Alt Text box, enter **Items in Stock** and click the Enter button ( ) or press Enter or Return. The alternative text appears if a browser can't display the image.

(Whenever the Enter button appears after a text box or field, you must click the button or press Enter or Return on the keyboard to apply the value.)

14 Choose File > Save to save the Navbar.html file. When prompted to update the files that use the component, click OK. Close the Navbar.html file.

Now you'll test the link, to make sure that it works as you expect.

Testing a link

You can test your links using the Show in Browser button on the toolbar.

1 Return to the home page by clicking the Index.html page to make it active.

2 Click the Show in Browser button on the toolbar. Index.html opens in any browsers you have specified in the preferences.

3 Click the Items in Stock graphic. The Stock.html file opens in the browser window.

Clicking linked graphic   *Result*

4 Choose File > Save to save your changes. Close the file.

Creating anchors

In this section, you'll create a link from a bulleted item to its corresponding section later in the page. Anchors act as bookmarks to locations within the same page. You can create a single link that connects to a single anchor. Or you can create several links that point to a single anchor point.

Creating an anchor by pointing and shooting

Now you'll work with the Stock page and add links to it. You'll start by adding an anchor that links to a topic later on the page.

1 If necessary, click the Stock.html document window to make it active. You opened the file when you tested the link that you just created.

This text file describes the Vintage Guitar product line of acoustic and electric guitars, amps, pedals, and other equipment.

2 Using the text cursor, triple-click the second item in the bulleted list, "Electric Guitars," to select the line. You'll create an anchor from this item to the topic later on the page. Using an anchor lets viewers jump to the information without having to scroll.

It's best to place anchors in the flow of HTML text, in a layout text box, or in a table. (You can add a small layout text box to the layout grid to hold the anchor.) You'll get more consistent results if you put the anchor near the left margin of the page. You cannot anchor directly to a graphic because HTML does not yet support this feature; instead, place the anchor near the top left of the graphic.

3 Hold down Alt (Windows) or Command (Mac OS) and Alt/Command-drag from the selected text downward, without releasing the mouse button.

As you drag, a line appears in your document; a hook icon appears at the end of the line when you begin dragging and again when you set the anchor.

4 To scroll through the document, hold down the mouse button on the bottom border of the window, and continue holding down the button as the window starts scrolling. Release the mouse button when the line is over the Electric Guitars head.

An anchor icon appears. The Link tab in the Text Inspector becomes active and displays a unique anchor name. The point and shoot method is the easiest way to create an anchor.

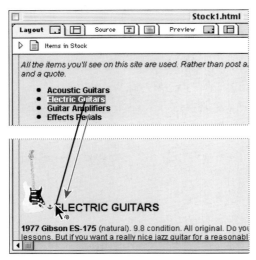

Alt/Command-dragging from bullet;
Anchor set in Electric Guitars head

Another way to create an anchor is using the Palette.

 5 Click the Basic tab (▣) of the Palette. Then drag the Anchor icon from the Palette to the third bulleted item, "Guitar Amplifiers."

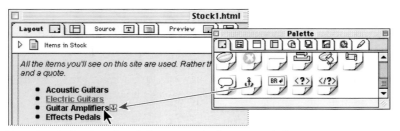

Dragging Anchor icon from Palette to text in document window

6 In the Anchor Inspector, enter a descriptive name for the anchor (we used "Amps"); then press Enter or Return. Naming anchors lets you update them more easily or find and correct broken links when you're managing your site.

7 In the document window, triple-click to select "Guitar Amplifiers." To link the anchor, Alt-drag (Windows) or Command-drag (Mac OS) from the selection to the head "Guitar Amplifiers," and release the mouse button. The document window springs back to where you set the beginning anchor.

8 Scroll down in the document to check that the ending anchor was inserted correctly.

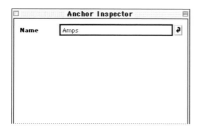

Naming anchor in Anchor Inspector

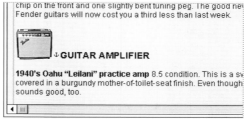

Anchor set in Guitar Amplifiers head

9 Create an anchor for the fourth bulleted item, "Effects Pedals," using either technique you just learned.

(If you'd like to make the bulleted list visually consistent, you can also create an anchor for the first bulleted item, "Acoustic Guitars," using either technique you just learned.)

10 Choose File > Save to save your file.

Verifying anchors

You've tried out previewing links using the Preview view in Adobe GoLive. You can also see how links and anchors work in a Web browser, by opening the file in a browser and testing the hyperlinks. Now you'll preview the anchors you just created.

1 Click the Show in Browser button in the upper right corner of the toolbar. The document appears in the Web browser you specified in the Preferences dialog box.

Show in Browser button

2 Click the bulleted text to see how the link jumps to the corresponding heads in the document.

3 When you have finished previewing, close or quit your browser. Then click the document window to return to the Stock.html file.

4 Close all open files except Stock.html.

Creating hypertext links

Now you'll create some hypertext links. You'll select some text in the Stock page and link the text to another page. The technique is similar to creating a graphic link or anchor.

1 In the document window, scroll to the bottom of the page. You'll create hypertext links from the last line in the document: "Home | Stock | Appraisals | Repairs."

2 Double-click the word "Home" to select it.

🖓 *Try these shortcuts when creating links: press Ctrl+L (Windows) or Command+L (Mac OS) to turn selected text into a link; press Ctrl/Command+Comma [,] to make the Link tab of the Inspector active and select the URL field; and press Ctrl/Command+Semicolon [;] to reselect the selected text in the document.*

3 Click the New Link button (⊂⊃) in the toolbar. The Inspector changes to the Text Inspector.

You'll create your first hypertext link using the Point and Shoot button in the Text Inspector to link to a file in the site window.

4 In the Link tab in the Text Inspector, position the pointer on the Point and Shoot button (◎).

5 Drag from the Point and Shoot button in the Text Inspector to Index.hmtl in the site window.

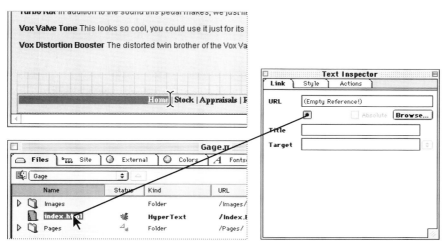

Creating link from Home text to Index.html file using point and shoot method

If the Index.html file isn't visible, position the pointer over the icon to the right of the Gage folder name until the Gage folder opens; drag to select the file, and then release the mouse button.

6 If you make a mistake, select the Home text in the document window and click the Remove Link icon (c/⊃) in the toolbar. Then repeat steps 3 through 5 to create the link.

You can also use the Remove Link button to unlink graphics.

You've just created a link to another file within the site. You can also create a link to files outside the site.

Create a link by browsing

Now you'll create a link to another file within the site by using the Inspector's Browse button to locate a file.

1 Select the text "Appraisals." Then click the New Link button (co) in the toolbar.

2 In the Text Inspector, click the Browse button and navigate to Appraise.html, located in the Gage/Pages/Appraise.html. Click Open.

Another way to specify a link in the Inspector is to enter the file's pathname in the URL text box. Now you'll create the final hypertext link.

3 Select the "Repairs" text in the document window. Click the New Link button (⬚) in the toolbar. In the Link tab in the Text Inspector, use any of these techniques to set the link destination:

• Drag from the Point and Shoot button to the Repairs.html file inside the Gage/Pages folder in the site window.

• Click the Browse button and navigate to Repairs.html in the Gage/Pages folder. Click Open.

• Enter the file's relative pathname in the URL text box: **../../Repairs.html.**

When you browse for the link destination or enter the URL, you can enter just the relative path (with the site folder name implied). Absolute URLs include the complete pathname of a file, including the site folder name. Relative URLs don't include the full pathname, and can refer to a file in a subdirectory from which the file is linked. By default, Adobe GoLive is aware of the site folder, so you don't need to enter it in the URL.

Adobe GoLive lets you decide whether the path specifications within URLs that refer to other items in site subfolders should be relative or absolute. This feature accommodates applications in which path specifications must be relative to the root folder of the site. It also allows Adobe GoLive to import sites that use absolute URLs without producing multiple error messages. For more information on absolute and relative paths, see "Setting up absolute paths" on page 135.

4 Choose File > Save to save the Stock.html file.

5 To preview the link you just created, click the Preview tab. In Preview view, click the Home, Appraisals, and Repairs links to test them. Each file opens in its own window.

You can also try out these links in your browser by clicking the Show in Browser button in the toolbar, and then clicking a link to test it. (If you've connected each link correctly, the information it's linked to appears in the document window. If not, the browser will display an error message.)

Close all open files except Stock.html. Then click the Layout tab (⬚) in the Stock.html document window to return to Layout view.

Setting up absolute paths

Adobe GoLive lets you decide whether the path specifications within URLs that refer to other items in sub-folders of the site folder should be relative or absolute. This lets you specify paths relative to the root site folder. It also lets Adobe GoLive import sites that use absolute URLs without generating multiple error messages.

Example: *The page /root/pages/info/page.html contains the image /root/images/image.gif, where root is the name of the site folder you specify when you save the site for the first time.*

By default, the URL in the referencing HTML page isn't aware of the presence of the root folder. This is reflected by the up one folder level notation—two periods, followed by a slash (../).

If you use relative paths, the path specification reads:

../../images/image.gif

This instructs the browser to go up two folder levels to locate the image file in the folder images.

If you use absolute paths, Adobe GoLive omits the up one folder level notation. This works only when the site is served by a Web server application, because the browser depends on the root directory information supplied by the server.

The absolute path specification would read:

/images/image.gif

This instructs the browser to locate the image file in the subfolder images within the root folder specified by the Web server.

Note that using absolute paths limits your previewing options. Pages aren't displayed properly when you choose the Show In Browser command to launch a Web browser for previewing. The browser reads the pages directly from the hard disk and would need a Web server application to supply it with information on the root directory and assist it in resolving the URLs.

Specifying absolute paths for referenced files

Adobe GoLive gives you two options for using absolute paths. You can use absolute paths for any new link or file reference you create throughout the application in the URL Handling General Preferences dialog box. Or you can set the absolute path option for individual links or file references.

As soon as you select Absolute, the up one level notations disappear from the Source text box. The reference to the image file is now absolute.

The Absolute option is turned off when you select a URL pointing at an external destination or an item that maintains a link across volumes.

Setting up Adobe GoLive to use absolute paths

You can set up Adobe GoLive to use absolute paths in the General URL Handling Preferences dialog box by selecting Make New Links Absolute.

–From the Adobe GoLive User Guide, Chapter 14

Changing a link's color and highlight

Now that you've created some links, you'll see how easy it is to change their color. You use the Page Inspector to change a link's color and highlight.

1 Click the Page icon (▤) in the upper left corner of the Stock.html document window, beneath the Layout tab. The Inspector changes to the Page Inspector.

Clicking Page icon to display Page Inspector

2 Click the Link color field to display the Color Palette, if it's not already open. In the Color Palette, click the Web I tab (●). This tab lets you select Web-safe colors for consistent color across platforms and browsers.

3 In the Color Palette, select another color either by scrolling or by entering a value. The color you choose should provide enough contrast between the page's background and text color so that it stands out, but not so much that it's distracting to the viewer.

4 Drag the color from the preview pane of the Color Palette to the Link color field in the Page Inspector. Notice that the Link option in the Page Inspector is now selected.

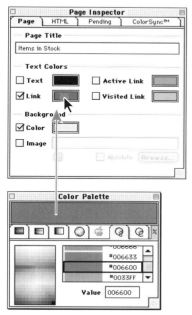

Dragging color from Color Palette preview pane to Link color field in Page Inspector

5 Repeat steps 3 and 4 for the Active Link and Visited Link color fields, selecting each field in turn.

When selecting a color for visited links, it's helpful to viewers to pick a color that's opposite the link color on the color wheel. So, for example, if the link color is red, you could use green for the visited link color.

6 Choose File > Save to save your work.

7 To preview the link color and how it changes when the link is clicked, click the Show in Browser button in the upper right corner of the toolbar. The document appears in your Web browser.

8 In the browser, scroll to the end of the document and click the Appraisals link to test it. Notice how the color changes when you click the link (the active link color), and after you've clicked it (the visited link color). To preview the visited link color, you must preview the document in a Web browser.

Note: Depending on how they've set browser preferences, some viewers won't be able to see the link colors that you've set.

9 When you have finished testing the links, close or quit your browser.

10 Click the Stock.html document window to return to the file.

Creating an action

You can add actions to links that increase their interactivity. For example, you can use actions that cause clicking a link to open a second window. Or you can add an action that displays or hides information when the viewer's pointer is over a link. You can also add an e-mail action to a link that lets viewers send comments.

Now you'll link the Custom Acoustic Guitar text on the Stock page to a guitar image. Then you'll add an action to the link that opens a second window at a preset size with that image.

1 In the Stock.html page, in the first paragraph of the Acoustic Guitar section, select the text "1927 Martin 0-28K."

Keep in mind that text used as a link should be short and descriptive. Try to keep the text to no more than five words—so that it captures the viewers' attention without requiring too much effort. If you inadvertently select too much text for a link, you can unlink the extraneous text using the Remove Link button.

First you'll set the link. You must first create a link in the Link tab in the Text Inspector before you can create an action associated with the link. Otherwise, the action you create will display an error message, "Empty URL."

2 Click the New Link button ( ) in the toolbar.

3 Drag from the Point and Shoot button ( ) in the Link tab to the Martin.html file in the site window, located in the Gage/Pages folder.

Now you'll add the action to the link.

4 In the Text Inspector, click the Actions tab.

5 In the Events pane, select Mouse Click. Then click the + button to activate the ?Action menu.

6 From the ?Action pop-up menu, choose Link > Open Window.

Selecting Link > Open Window action

7 In the Open Window dialog box, click Browse, and locate the 1927martin.jpg image file in the Gage/Images folder. Click Open.

8 For size, enter 170 in the first text box and 325 in the second text box. Deselect Resize, Scroll, Menu, and Dir. You don't want the second window to resize, be scrollable, have a menu, or show a directory toolbar in some browsers.

9 Choose File > Save to save the file.

10 To test the action, start your browser and open the Stock.html file, inside the Gage/Pages folder. Try out the action by clicking the "1927 Martin 0-28K" text. Then close your browser.

Previewing Open Window action

11 Close the 1927martin.jpg and Stock.html files.

Using clickable image maps

Clickable image maps are images with clickable hot spots. You can link image maps to other resources and connect the hot spot areas in the map to other scripted actions such as forms or mailing addresses.

Now you're ready to work on the final page of your site. You'll add a clickable image map to an image of a guitar, and link the hot spot areas in the map to other pages. You'll start by opening the page in which you'll create the image map.

1 In the site window, double-click Repairs.html, inside the Gage/Pages folder, to open the file.

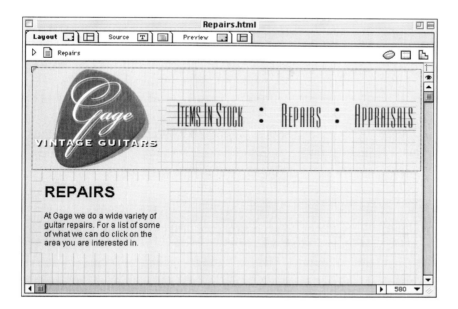

Now you'll insert the image for your image map.

2 Drag the Image icon from the Basic tab (□) of the Palette to the document window so that the placeholder is centered beneath the Navbar component. It's unnecessary to resize the placeholder, because it will resize automatically when you insert the image.

3 If necessary, click the Basic tab in the Image Inspector.

You use the Image Inspector to insert an image into the Repairs.html file. The technique for inserting an image is similar to adding a link.

4 Insert the Map.gif image, located in the Gage/Images folder within the Gage folder, using any of these techniques:

• Drag from the Point and Shoot button (⊚) to Map.gif located in the Gage/Images folder in the site window.

• Click Browse and navigate to the Map.gif file inside the Gage/Images folder, and click Open.

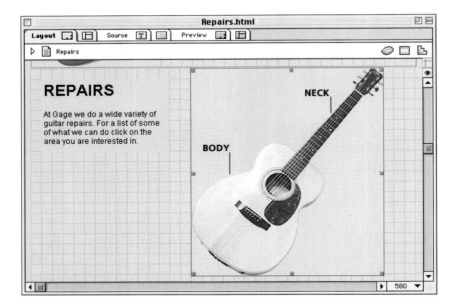

5 If necessary, drag the image to reposition it under the Navbar component.

Creating hot spots on an image map

You'll use the Guitar image to show specific repairs that guitars might need. First you'll create hot spots for the types of repairs on the guitar. Then you'll create a link from the hot spot to information on repair stores.

You'll start by getting rid of the border around the image.

1 With the image selected, click the Spec. (Special) tab of the Image Inspector. Select the Border option and enter **0**. In the Alt Text box, type **Repair map**, and press Enter or Return. This alternative text appears if a browser can't display the image.

2 Click the Map tab in the Image Inspector. Then select the Use Map option. This option lets you add an image map to an image and activates the tools in the Palette tab.

You use the Map tab to create an image map. The Map tab also contains drawing tools for creating the hot spots of an image map.

3 In the Map Name text box, enter a name for the map, and the suffix **.map**. (We named the map "Guitar.map.")

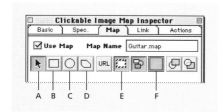

A. Pointer button B. Rectangle Region button
C. Circle Region button D. Polygon Region button
E. Frame Region button F. Select Color button

4 Click the rectangular Region Tool button. (Tooltips identifying the icons appear as you move the pointer over the tools in the Map tab toolbar.)

5 In the document window, drag a rectangular area that includes all of the guitar neck. Handles appear at the sides and corners of the hot spot. You can use these handles to adjust the hot spot or simply drag the hot spot to reposition it.

(For a more precise hot spot, draw it using the polygon region tool.)

6 In the Map tab, click the circular Region Tool button. In the document window, drag a circular hot spot over the guitar body that overlaps the rectangular hot spot.

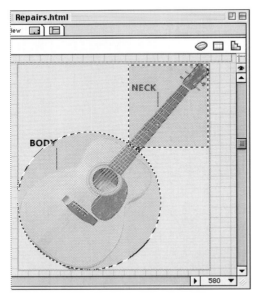

Overlapping rectangular and circular hot spots   *Hot-spot drawing tools in Map tab*

Editing hot spots

You can edit an image map's hot-spot area to change its shape, color, or border, as well as reposition hots spots and change how they overlap. Now you'll change the hot spots' color and positioning.

1 Click the Select Color button (the third button from the right); then select a different fill color for the hot spot. (Blue is the default.)

2 Drag the color from the preview pane of the Color Palette to the Select Color button in the Map tab.

Dragging color from preview pane of Color Palette to Select Color button

3 If desired, click the Frame Regions button (the fifth button from the right) in the Map tab in the Clickable Image Map Inspector to turn off or on the border around the hot spot.

You can change how hot spots overlap when a hot spot in front covers another behind it, by selecting one of the hot spots and clicking either the Bring Region to Front or Send Region to Back button.

Instead, you'll reposition the hot spots so that they don't overlap.

4 In the Map tab in the Clickable Image Map Inspector, click the Pointer Tool button (the leftmost button). In the document window, click the rectangular hot spot to select it. Handles appear around the hot spot.

5 Drag the handles of the rectangular hot spot to adjust it so that it no longer overlaps the circular hot spot.

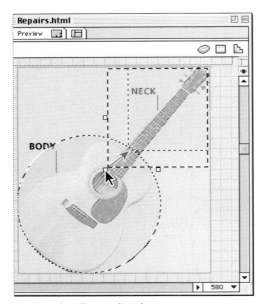

Dragging handles to adjust hot spots

Linking a clickable map with a Web page

Linking a clickable map with a Web page uses a technique similar to creating a hypertext link.

1 Select the rectangular hot spot.

2 In the Map tab in the Clickable Image Map Inspector, link the rectangular hot spot to the Neck.html file using any of these techniques:

• Drag from the Point and Shoot button (⌾) to the Neck.html file, located in the Gage/Repair_Pages folder, in the site window. (If needed, position the pointer on the folder name in the site window to open the folder; then release the mouse button when the contents of the Repair_Pages folder appears.)

• Click Browse and navigate to the Neck.html file Gage/Repair_Pages folder, and click Open.

• In the URL text box, type the URL **Repair_Pages/Neck.html**, and press Enter or Return. (It's OK to use a relative pathname.)

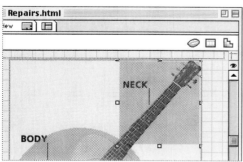

Rectangular hot spot in Repair.html

Link to Neck.html in Clickable Image Map Inspector

3 Repeat steps 1 and 2 to link the circular hot spot to the Body.html file in the Gage/Repair_Pages folder.

4 Choose File > Save to save the Repair.html file.

5 To test the hot spot, in the document window, click the Preview tab and click the hot spot. When you have finished previewing them, close the Neck.html and Body.html files.

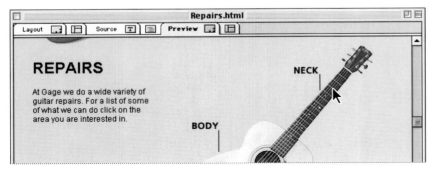

Clicking hot spot

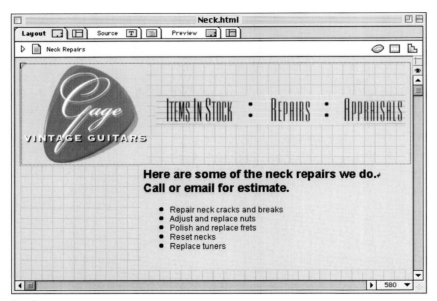

Result

6 Click the Layout tab to return to Layout view.

Setting preferences for link warnings

You can control the appearance of link warnings, including their text and background color and box size. The default color for broken links is red.

1 Choose Edit > Preferences.

2 On the left side of the Preferences dialog box, click the icon next to the General option to display more options. Click the Display option.

3 To select a different color for link warnings, click the Link Warning color field. The system color picker appears.

4 Select a color palette, select a color, and then click OK.

5 To set the size of the color box that marks link warnings in the text or around images, choose an option from the Frame Border pop-up menu. Click OK.

6 Choose File > Save to save the file and close the Repairs.html file.

Finding and fixing broken links

In this final exercise, you'll fix some broken links located on the Index.html page. By default broken links appear outlined in red in the Document window and in the Inspector URL text box.

1 Double-click the Navbar.html file, in the Extra tab of the site window. This file contains several broken links. (You can also locate the file in the Gage/Gage.data/Components folder, and open it from the desktop.

2 Click the Layout tab (▭) of the Navbar.html file to display it in Layout view.

3 To turn on the display of link warnings, click the Link Warnings button (▨) in the toolbar or choose Edit > Show Link Warnings.

Images with broken links appear with a border in the color you set in the previous section for the link warnings.

4 Select the Repairs image in the document window.

5 Click the Link tab in the Image Inspector. Notice that the link appears broken, as indicated by the highlight color in the URL text box and the bug icon next to the Point and Shoot button.

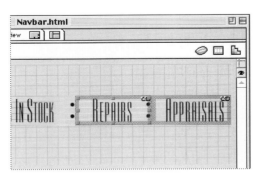

Broken link

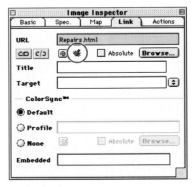

Link tab of Image Inspector

6 In the Link tab, locate the page that the Repairs button should be linked to by dragging from the Point and Shoot button to the Repairs.html file, inside the Pages folder, in the site window.

You'll repeat these last steps to relink the Appraisals button image to the corresponding file.

7 Select the Appraisals button image in the document window. This link also appears broken in the Link tab in the Image Inspector.

8 Now relink this image to the Appraise.html file by dragging from the Point and Shoot button in the Link tab to the Appraise.html file, inside the Pages folder, in the site window.

9 Choose File > Save to save the file. When prompted to update the file, click OK.

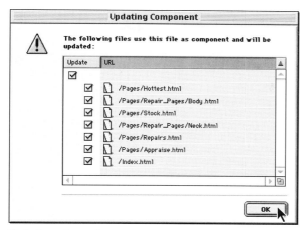

Updating a dynamic component

10 Close the Navbar.html file.

Previewing links

As a final step, you should ensure that your links all work as you expect by previewing them in your browser.

1 Start your browser.

2 Locate and open your completed Index.html file:

• On Windows, choose File > Open. Select the Index.html file, located in the Lesson03/03Start/Gage Folder/Gage folder, inside the Lessons folder on your hard drive, and click Open.

• On Mac OS, choose File > Open. Select the Index.html file, located in the Lesson03/03Start/Gage *f* /Gage folder, inside the Lessons folder on your hard drive, and click Open.

3 Click the links in the Index.html file, and explore the site.

4 When you have finished viewing the file, close it.

5 Close and quit your browser.

This concludes the linking lesson. For additional practice in fixing broken links, see Lesson 8, "Site Management."

Review questions

1 What is a hyperlink? How do you create a hyperlink?

2 What is an anchor? How do you create one?

3 What is the best location for an anchor?

4 How do you add an action to a link?

5 How do you create a link in a dynamic component?

6 What is the difference between relative and absolute pathnames. Why is this difference significant for links?

7 What is a clickable image map and how do you create one?

8 What is the purpose of a link warning?

9 How do you display all of the contents of the site window?

Review answers

1 A hyperlink is a jump from one location in a document to another location in a document—on the same page (called an anchor), locally within a site, across the Web, or to non-Web resources such as FTP servers, newsgroups, and e-mail addresses.

You create a hyperlink from text or an image by selecting it in the document window, and then clicking the New Link button in the toolbar. You then click the Link tab in the Inspector and use the Point and Shoot button or Browse button to link to another file in the site, or enter the file pathname in the URL text box.

You can also use keyboard shortcuts to create a link: Press Ctrl+L (Windows) or Command+L (Mac OS) to turn selected text into a link; press Ctrl/Command+Comma [,] to make the Link tab of the Inspector active and select the URL field; and press Ctrl/Command+Semicolon [;] to reselect the selected text in the document.

2 Anchors act as bookmarks to locations within the same page. You can create a single link that connects to a single anchor. Or you can create several links that point to a single anchor point.

To create an anchor from one location on the page to another, you select text or drag an Anchor icon from the Palette to the text in the document window. Then you Alt-drag (Windows) or Command-drag (Mac OS) to the link destination on the page. You can use the Anchor Inspector to name the anchor.

3 It's best to place anchors in the flow of HTML text, in a layout text box, or in a table. (You can add a small layout text box to the layout grid to hold the anchor.) You'll get more consistent results if you put the anchor near the left margin of the page. You cannot anchor directly to a graphic because HTML does not yet support this feature; instead, place the anchor near the top left of the graphic.

4 To add an action to a link, you first make a selection and create a link using the New Link button in the toolbar or in the Link tab in the Text Inspector. Then you use the Actions tab in the Inspector to add an action to the link.

5 A dynamic component updates all files that refer to it whenever a change is made to the component. Adding a link to a dynamic component uses the same technique as other hyperlinks, but requires that you first open the dynamic component file.

6 Absolute URLs include the complete pathname of a file, including the site folder name. Relative URLs don't include the full pathname, and can refer to a file in a subdirectory from which the file is linked. When you browse for the link destination or enter the URL, you can enter just the relative path (with the site folder name implied). By default, Adobe GoLive is aware of the site folder, so you don't need to enter it in the URL.

7 Clickable image maps are images with clickable hot spots. You can link image maps to other resources and connect the hot spot areas in the map to other scripted actions such as forms or mailing addresses. To create a clickable image map, you insert an image in your document, specify the image as an image map using the Map tab in the Image Inspector, and add hot spots using tools in the Map tab. You then add links to the hot spots as you would any other hyperlink.

8 Link warnings appear as a highlighted URL text box in the Link tab of the Inspector (or as bug icons in the site window). Link warnings alert you to files with broken links that require fixing before uploading the files to a Web server (and frustrating viewers who can't find the hyperlinked information).

9 To expand the view of the site window, use these techniques:

• In Windows, click the icon at the bottom left of the site window to display all of the site contents. At the top of the split site window, click the Extra tab to display the site's Gage.data folder and its contents. (You may have to drag the site window up to display all of its contents.) Double-click the Components folder to open it; then double-click the Navbar.html file to open it.

• In Mac OS, click the icon leftmost in the title bar of the site window to display all of the site contents. On the left side of the split screen, click the Extra tab to display the site's Gage.data folder and its contents. Double-click the Components folder to open it; then double-click the Navbar.html file to open it.

Lesson 4

4 Working with Frames

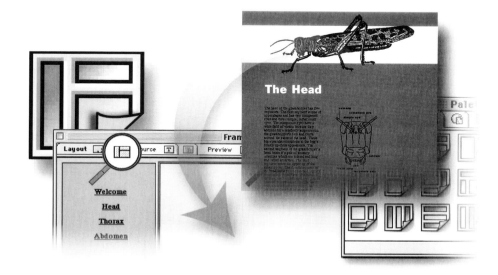

Frames are very useful for controlling the layout and structure of your site. They can be used both as a navigation tool and to show more than one type of information at the same time. In this lesson, you will create a frame set with three frames and add their content.

In this lesson you'll learn how to do the following:

- Create a page for your frame set.
- Create a frame set.
- Change frame set options using the Frame Set Inspector.
- Configure individual frames using the Frame Inspector.
- Add, move, and delete a frame.
- Add content to frames.
- Create targeted links within the frame set.
- Link the frame set to your home page.

This lesson will take you about an hour to complete. If necessary, remove the previous lesson from your desktop and copy the Lesson04 folder onto it.

About frame sets

A frame set is an HTML page that holds several frames and that allows you to show a different document in each frame. Using a frame structure, you can display several HTML documents at once, each in its own pane within the browser window. Each pane works independently and can be scrollable or static, depending on its purpose.

A frame set does not contain the individual HTML pages that are displayed. It simply provides them with a structure. If you look at the source code for a page containing a frame set, it just has basic HTML meta-information and a few lines of code defining the frame set—nothing else.

The simplest frame set contains two frames, one for navigation purposes and one to display content. The one you will create in this lesson will have three: a Navigation frame, a main page frame, and a banner image frame.

Note: *You will not be nesting frame sets in this lesson. While this is allowed in HTML, it can cause serious navigational problems.*

Structure of the frame set

In this lesson, you will be creating the following frame set:

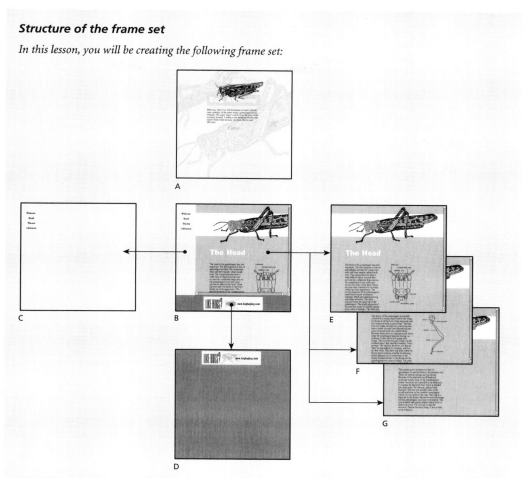

A. *Index.html* **B.** *Frameset.html* **C.** *Nav.html* **D.** *Banner.html* **E.** *Head.html* **F.** *Thorax.html* **G.** *Abdomen.html*

You will create the frame set titled Frameset.html, then import the various content pages into it, as shown in the diagram.

Getting started

In this lesson, you'll create a frame set for a Web site called BugBody, then add the content to the frames. First, you'll view the finished Web site in your browser.

1 Open your browser.

2 Open the 04End folder in the 04Lesson.

3 Open the BugBody Folder (Windows) or the Bugbody *f* folder (Mac OS); then open the Bugbody folder.

4 Open Index.html. This is the site's home page. As it is not part of the frame set, it appears as one page across the whole browser.

5 Click Enter. This link is to an HTML page called Frameset.html. Although you can see content in this page, Frameset.html only contains code for the site's frame set. The content pages open up inside the frame set.

Notice that the page has three frames: the information about the grasshopper's head is the main frame; the list of contents is another frame; and the animated image at the bottom of the page is another.

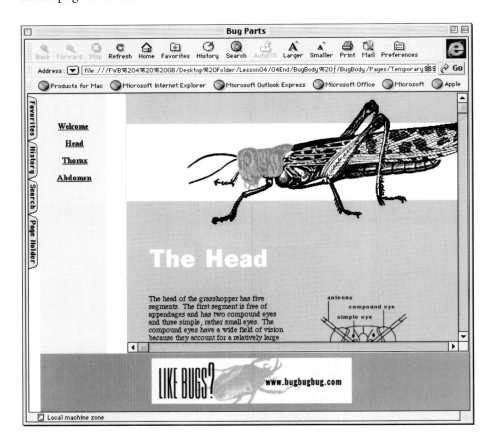

6 Click the links in the list of contents and explore the site.

7 When you have finished viewing the site, quit your browser.

Creating a frame set

When you create a new Web site using frames, you need to set up the page containing your frame set first, then carefully consider how you want the frames to look. Only then should you start adding and formatting your content pages.

You will begin this lesson by opening the BugBody Web site and creating a new HTML page containing a frame set.

1 Start Adobe GoLive.

2 Open the 04Start folder in the 04Lesson.

3 Open the BugBody Folder (Windows) or the Bugbody *f* folder (Mac OS); then open the BugBody.site file (Windows) or the BugBody.π file (Mac OS).

This site contains a home page (Index.html) and several content pages. These pages are not currently set out in frames. You will create a frame set for the site's content pages.

4 In Untitled.html, change the Page Title field next to the Page icon (📄) to **Bug Parts**.

5 Choose File > Save to save the page as **Frameset.html**. (Save it in the 04Start > BugBody > Pages folder.)

Adding a frame set

Now that you've created a new page, you can add a frame set to it. When you work with frames, you start by selecting a frame set from the Palette and then configure it in the Frame Editor of the document window.

1 Click the Frame Editor tab (🗔) of the document window to display the Frame Editor. It currently says No Frames.

2 Click the Frames tab (🗖) of the Palette to select the tab.

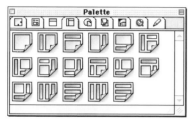

Frames tab of Palette

The Frames tab contains a variety of frame set templates, with up to three frames in them. Each template shows you how the frames will appear on the page.

Note: *The first icon on the top row shows just one frame. You can use this to add an additional frame to a frame set.*

 3 In the Frames tab of the Palette, select the fifth icon in the second row and drag it from the Frames tab to the Frame Editor. A frame set appears in the document window.

Note: *If you have resized your Palette, this icon may appear in a different position.*

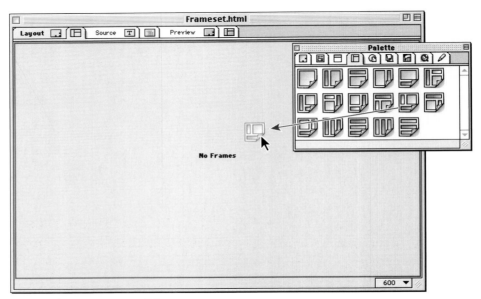

Dragging frame set to Frame Editor

Notice that each frame contains the words "No Name" and has a question mark icon in it with the words "Empty Reference!" under it. You will name each frame and fill it with content later in this lesson. But now is a good time to take a look at the source code for the new frame set.

4 Click the Source tab of the document window (☐T☐) to display the Source view. The source code for this page consists solely of the frame tags and some meta-information.

5 Return to the Frame Editor.

Making changes to the frame set

You can make several changes to a frame set, such as changing its orientation or borders, by using the Frame Set Inspector.

1 Click the internal border above the bottom frame to open the Frame Set Inspector.

You can select any internal border of the frame set to open the Frame Set Inspector.

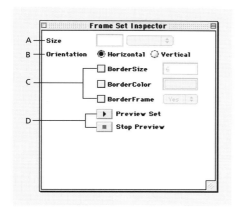

A. Size *B. Orientation* *C. Border properties*
D. Preview buttons

2 Select the Horizontal Orientation option and notice how this changes the appearance of the frames on both sides of the selected border. Then reselect the Vertical Orientation option.

Note: These options do not change the orientation of the entire frame set, but only of the frames adjacent to the selected border.

3 Select the BorderSize option and enter **5** in the text box. Press Enter or Return, or click the return button ( ) to enter the new border size. Notice how the change only applies to the border you selected to open the Frame Set Inspector.

4 Select the BorderColor option and click the gray color field to open the Color Palette.

5 Select the Real Web Colors tab ( ) on the Color Palette and select a color. (We entered 99CC99 in the Value field.) This fills the top Color Preview pane with your selected color.

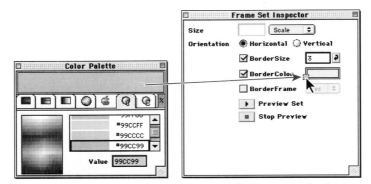

Selecting color from Color Palette   *Dragging color to BorderColor field in Frame Set Inspector*

6 Drag this color from the Color Preview pane of the Color Palette to the BorderColor field on the Frame Set Inspector. Notice how this changes *all* the internal borders.

7 Close the Color Palette.

8 Select the internal border between the top two frames.

Notice that this frame is set to a horizontal orientation. Select the Vertical Orientation option to see how this affects the orientation of the frames; then return to Horizontal Orientation.

9 Select the BorderSize option and enter **0** in the text box. Then select BorderFrame and select No from the pop-up menu. The border will not appear in a browser, although you can still see a black line in the Frame Editor.

Note: *Many Web designers use borderless frames with the same background color to give the impression of a frameless Web site.*

10 Choose File > Save to save your work.

Setting up the main content frame

You will use the Frame Inspector to name the main content frame in your set, resize it, and add a scrollbar.

1 Select the top left frame. This opens the Frame Inspector.

The Frame Inspector is context sensitive and lets you specify options for a selected frame. You can resize and name it, link it to a content page, and set its scrolling and resizing properties. You can also turn content viewing on or off.

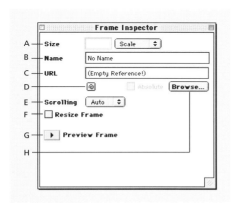

A. Size *B.* Name *C.* URL typed entry
D. Point and Shoot button to URL link
E. Scrolling *F.* Resize *G.* Preview button
H. Browse to URL link

2 In the Name text box of the Frame Inspector, name the frame **Navigator**.

Now, you'll set the size of the frame. You can do this in several ways:

• Drag the borders to where you want them.

• Enter a precise pixel size for each pane.

• Enter a percentage of the browser window for each pane.

• Make a frame scale to fit the browser window.

You will set the size of the Navigation frame to a precise pixel size. Because this frame will contain a navigation bar, it should be the same width in all browsers and at all screen resolutions, to ensure that the wording for the links can be seen at all times.

3 Resize the frame by selecting Pixel in the Size pop-up menu and entering 110 in the Size text box. Notice that the left-hand frame is now slightly larger than it was.

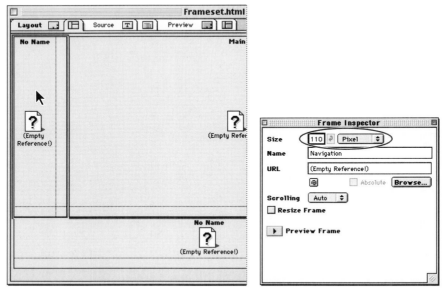

Selecting pixel size for Navigation frame   Navigation frame

4 Leave Resize Frame deselected. This prevents viewers from changing the layout of your frames.

5 Choose No from the Scrolling pop-up menu to make the pane nonscrolling.

A navigational pane is more useful if it's nonscrolling. Rather than force site viewers to scroll through links, you should cut the pane's content. If your site has too many pages to show on the navigation pane, consider reorganizing the site into areas, and use the navigation pane to take a viewer to those areas, rather than straight to individual pages. Each area can have its own Contents list, showing its pages.

Now, you will format the main content frame.

6 Select the top right frame. In the Frame Inspector, select Scale from the Size field pop-up menu.

If a viewer resizes the browser window, the Scale option allows this frame to expand or contract to fill all of the browser window to the right of the Navigation frame.

7 In the Name text box, name the frame **Main**.

8 Choose Yes from the Scrolling pop-up menu. This will add vertical and horizontal scrollbars to the frame.

Now, you will format the bottom frame.

9 Select the bottom frame and name it **Banner**.

10 Set its size to 90 pixels. This is slightly larger than the image that will fill this frame, to allow for shifting in different browsers.

11 Choose the No Scrolling option.

12 Choose File > Save to save your work.

Adding, moving, and deleting frames

You can add frames to the frame set, move them around, and delete them. First, you'll add a fourth frame to your set.

 1 In the Frames tab of the Palette, drag a new frame (the first icon on the top row) to the bottom frame of your frame set. It appears to the right of the existing frame.

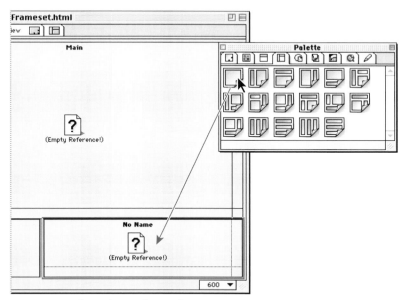

Dragging new frame from Palette to frame set

2 Now resize the frame by entering **20 percent** in the Size field in the Frame Inspector.

You will now move the new frame to the left of the original frame.

3 Drag the new frame over the original bottom frame until it turns black (Windows) or gray (Mac OS), then drop it onto the frame. The new frame appears to the left of the original one.

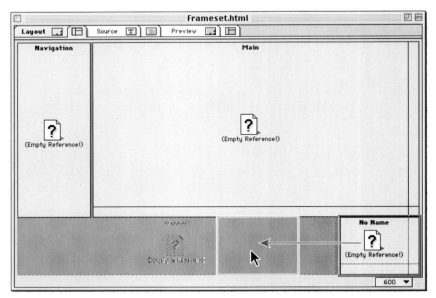

Dragging new frame to left of original one

Now, you will delete the frame you have just added.

4 Select the new frame and press Delete. This removes the new frame and resizes the original frame to 50 percent of the page.

5 Select the bottom frame and re-enter **90 pixels** in the Size field to return the Banner pane to its original size.

Adding content to frames

It's time to add content to each of your three frames by linking them to content pages. You'll do this in several ways:

• By using the Browse button in the Frame Inspector.

• By using the Point and Shoot button () in the Frame Inspector.

• By dragging and dropping a content file directly into a frame.

You're going to use each method as you add content to the three frames.

First, you'll browse for a file. This technique is particularly useful if the content file does not reside in the same folder as the rest of your Web site.

1 Select the Navigation frame on the left of the page. In the Frame Inspector, browse to Nav.html in your Web site. Click Open. An icon representing the file appears in the frame.

• On the Mac OS, click the Preview Frame button (▶) in the Frame Inspector. The contents list in Nav.html appears in the frame. (You can click the button again to turn off the display, but leave it on for now.)

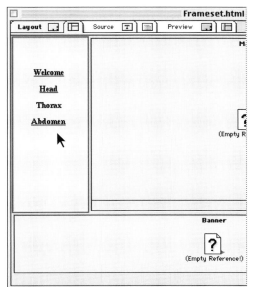

Select Navigation frame (Mac OS).

Click Preview Frame button in Frame Inspector.

💡 *If you find that a content page (such as the list of Contents) is too wide to show all the text in its frame, reformat the page after you set the frame size.*

Now, you'll try another technique for adding a content file. If the file resides in your Web site, you can use the Point and Shoot button in the Frame Inspector to add content to a frame.

2 If necessary, drag the document window to a place on your screen where you can see both the Main frame of your frame set and the files in your site window.

3 In the site window, open the Pages folder.

4 In the document window, select the Main frame. In the Frame Inspector, drag the Point and Shoot button (⊚) to the Head.html file in the site window to create a link.

5 Preview the contents of the frame. Notice how both a vertical and horizontal scrollbar appear on the frame.

The final method for adding content to a frame is perhaps the easiest. This is by dragging.

6 If necessary, drag the document window to a place on your screen where you can see both the bottom frame of your frame set and the files in your site window. (You may need to resize Frameset.html to do this.)

7 Drag Banner.html from your site window into the bottom frame. The image file is now linked to the frame.

8 Preview the contents of the frame.

Note: *When you want to add an image as the content of a frame, you must first put the image into an HTML page. A frame will not show a plain image file.*

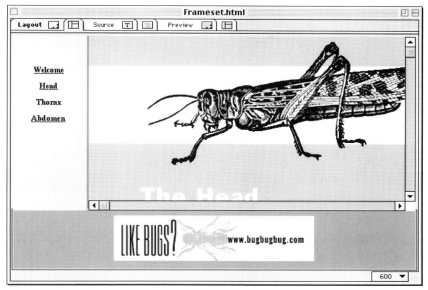

Previewing content of all three frames (Mac OS only)

9 Choose File > Save to save your frame set.

Creating targeted links

Although your frames can be used simply to display these three Web pages, they are much more powerful when used to navigate through and view your entire site. You will enable a viewer to change the content of the Main frame by using targeted links from the Navigation (contents) pane to other pages.

1 From the site window, open Nav.html.

2 In the Nav.html file, select the word Thorax.

3 Click the Link button on the Site toolbar (⊑).

4 In the Text Inspector, use the Point and Shoot button to create a link to Thorax.html.

This creates a link between the two pages. But which frame will it appear in? You want it to appear in the Main frame, so you must select that frame as the target.

5 In the Text Inspector, choose Main from the Target pop-up menu.

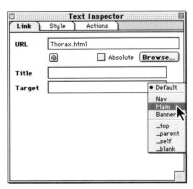

Selecting Main frame as target

Now, when a visitor clicks on this link in the Contents, Thorax.html will replace Head.html in the Main frame.

Creating a link back to the home page

You are going to target the Welcome link on this page to the home page. This will allow viewers to return to the home page at any time and from anywhere in your site.

1 Select the Welcome link.

2 In the site window, make sure that Index.html is visible.

3 In the Text Inspector, use the Point and Shoot button to create a link to Index.html.

4 This time, in the Text Inspector, choose _parent from the Target pop-up menu.

The _parent option specifies the browser window as the target and causes the browser to change the content of the entire window. The browser will replace the frame set with one pane that shows the home page; it will no longer display the navigation bar or banner.

The other two links have already been done for you.

5 Save and close the Nav.html file.

6 Choose File > Save to save Frameset.html.

7 Be sure that Frameset.html is selected, and not one of the frames inside it; then choose Special > Show in Browser > (your favorite browser) to open Frameset.html in your browser.

8 Click each of the links in the Contents pane (select the Welcome link last). The linked pages appear in the Main pane.

Notice that when you click the Welcome link, the site's home page fills the entire browser window. This shows the effect of setting the link's target to _parent. However, you will also notice that nothing happens when you click on Enter.

Linking the frame set to your home page

The final task you have is to create a link from your home page to the new frame set. This link usually says something like Enter. When a viewer clicks it, the frame set opens, displaying your site's opening content pages.

Note that you *don't* create a link to a content page; you create a link to Frameset.html, which will open showing the three content pages in its frames.

1 Close your browser.

2 In the site window, open Index.html.

3 Ensure that the site window is visible, and that the Pages folder is open.

4 In Index.html, select the text Enter.

5 Click the New Link button (CD) on the site toolbar. In the Text Inspector, use the Point and Shoot button to create a link to Frameset.html.

6 Choose File > Save to save Frameset.html.

Congratulations! You have created a three-frame view for your Web site and integrated an HTML page containing a frame set into it. If you wish, you can open it in your browser and see how it works.

Review questions

1 Where will you find a set of ready-made frame layouts?

2 How do you set a frame size to a specific number of pixels?

3 How do you add color to a frame border?

4 How do you add a scrollbar to a frame?

5 How do you add a new frame to your frame set?

6 What are the three ways to fill a frame with content?

7 How can you preview the content in your frame set without launching a browser?

Review answers

1 You will you find a set of ready-made frame layouts on the Frames tab of the Palette.

2 Select the frame. In the Frame Inspector, choose Pixel from the Size pop-up menu and enter the number of pixels in the Size text box.

3 Select the frame border. In the Frame Set Inspector, select the BorderColor option, and then click on the color field to open the Color Palette. Select the Real Web Colors tab and select the color you want. Drag it from the Color Preview pane of the Color Palette to the BorderColor color field.

4 Select a frame. In the Frame Inspector, choose Yes from the Scrolling pop-up menu.

5 Drag a Frame icon from the Frames tab of the Palette to your frame set. Drop it into the frame you want.

6 Select a frame. You can fill it with content:

• By browsing for a file in the Frame Inspector.

• By using the Point and Shoot button on the Frame Inspector to link to a file.

• By dragging a file from the site window to the frame.

7 Select the Preview tab on the site window, or double-click on the page icon in a frame to open its content file in another window.

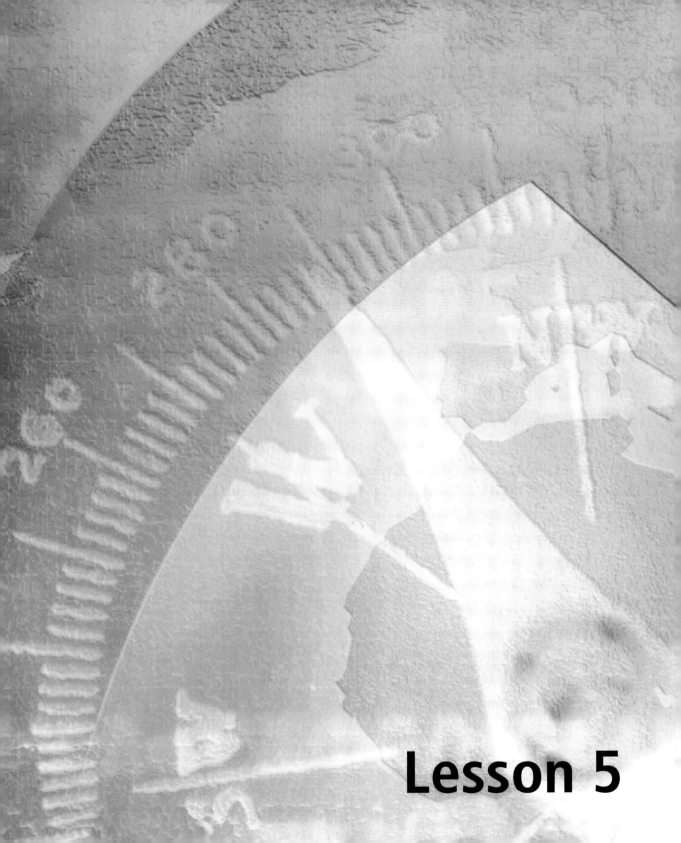

Lesson 5

5 | Animation

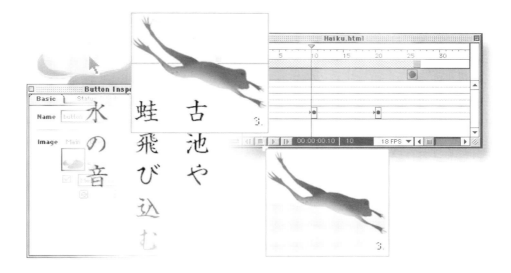

Adobe GoLive supports Dynamic HTML so you can add animation to your pages. You can create rollover buttons that change appearance as your mouse moves over them. In addition, DHTML lets you add floating boxes to Web pages. You can then animate those floating boxes to move their contents around the page. You can even make floating boxes that pass in front of and then behind each other as they move.

Getting started

In this lesson, you'll learn how to do the following:

- Create rollovers.
- Create floating boxes.
- Restack and fill floating boxes with text and images.
- Animate multiple floating boxes.
- Edit animations.
- Apply actions to floating boxes and Web pages.

This lesson will take about 60 minutes to complete.

If needed, remove the previous lesson folder from your hard drive and copy the Lesson05 folder onto it. As you work on this lesson, you'll overwrite the Start files. If you need to restore the Start files, copy them from the Adobe GoLive Classroom in a Book CD.

You'll begin this lesson by using your Web browser to view a copy of the finished Web pages.

1 Start a DHTML-compliant Web browser, such as Netscape Communicator 4 or Microsoft Internet Explorer 4. (If the browser is not compliant, features such as animation or actions will not be visible.)

2 Use the browser to open the Web page index.html:

- In Windows, the path is Lesson05/05End/Poetry Folder/Poetry/index.html.
- In Mac OS, the path is Lesson05/05End/Poetry ƒ /Poetry/index.html.

This site represents a work in progress, with a few active links.

3 Click the Poetry Sampler link at the top of the Web page index.html and the lotus flower link at the bottom of the page to explore the site.

4 When you have finished viewing the Web site, quit your browser.

Creating rollovers

In this first part of the lesson, you'll make a rollover button. Rollovers are objects that change their look as the mouse pointer passes over or clicks them.

1 Start Adobe GoLive.

An empty document called untitled.html opens in the document window. Because you will be opening an existing page from a site, you won't need this empty, untitled page.

2 Close the page untitled.html.

3 Choose File > Open and open the Poetry.site file:

• In Windows, the path is Lesson05/05Start/Poetry Folder/Poetry.site.

• In Mac OS, the path is Lesson05/05Start/Poetry ƒ /Poetry.π.

4 Double-click the file index.html in the site window to open the page.

Although you can use the JavaScript Editor in Adobe GoLive to create JavaScript rollovers from scratch, Adobe GoLive provides a button image *cyberobject* that makes this process much easier. A button image can be placed on a Web page, where it serves as a container for the images used for the different states of the rollover and a JavaScript that switches the images depending on the location of the mouse pointer. In this lesson, you'll create a rollover using a button image cyberobject.

5 If necessary, choose View > Inspector (Windows) or Window > Inspector (Mac OS) to display the Inspector.

6 If necessary, choose View > Palette (Windows) or Window > Palette (Mac OS) to display the Palette.

7 Click the CyberObjects tab (⬚) in the Palette.

8 Drag the Button Image icon from the Palette to the top left corner of the layout grid on the page.

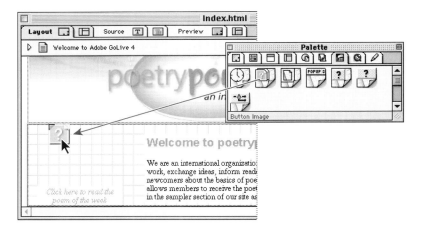

Notice that the Inspector changes to the Button Inspector. Notice, too, that the Main icon is selected in the Button Inspector. This indicates that the button image placeholder is ready to be linked to the image you want shown when the mouse pointer is not over the button—in other words, its main state.

9 Drag from the Point and Shoot button ( ) in the Button Inspector to the file Week_main.jpg in the Media folder in the site window.

Note: *In Windows, you can drag from the Point and Shoot button to a closed folder to open it.*

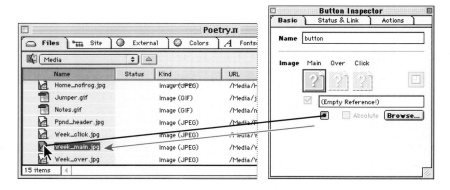

The image you selected (a closed lotus flower) replaces the Button Image icon in the Web page and the Main icon in the Button Inspector.

10 If necessary, drag the image to the right to center it over the text "Click here to read the poem of the week."

Next, you'll specify the image that will appear when a visitor's pointer is *over* the button in the Web page.

11 Click the Over icon in the Button Inspector. Then click the Navigation frame next to the text box in the Image area of the Button Inspector to display the Point and Shoot button.

12 Drag from the Point and Shoot button to the file Week_over.jpg in the Media folder in the site window.

Because you are in Layout view, the button on the Web page still shows the main image for the rollover. However, the Week_over.jpg image replaces the Over icon in the Button Inspector.

Now you'll apply the image that will appear when the rollover is clicked.

13 Click the Click icon in the Button Inspector. Then click the Navigation frame next to the text box in the Image area to display the Point and Shoot button.

14 Drag from the Point and Shoot button to the file Week_click.jpg in the Media folder in the site window.

You've just created a rollover in Adobe GoLive. Now you'll link it to another page, so that clicking the rollover moves you to the page.

15 Click the Status & Link tab in the Button Inspector.

16 In the Button Inspector, click the Navigation frame next to URL to activate the Point and Shoot button. Then drag from the Point and Shoot button to the page Forever.html in the Pages folder in the site window.

17 Choose File > Save.

You can preview the rollover with your Web browser.

18 Click the triangle next to the Show in Browser menu in the toolbar and choose a Web browser from the menu. For information on setting up Web browsers, see "Previewing Web pages with Adobe GoLive" on page 23.

19 In the Web browser, notice that moving the pointer over the button and clicking it displays the different states of the rollover and moves you to another page.

Note: Depending on the speed of the Internet connection and the browser used, the "mouse click" state of the image may not appear.

Pointer away from   *Pointer on button*   *Button clicked*
button

20 Close the Web page index.html in the browser and then close it in Adobe GoLive.

Working with floating boxes

Newer browsers, such as Internet Explorer 4 and Netscape Communicator support Hypertext Markup Language (HTML) 4.0 and Dynamic Hypertext Markup Language (DHTML). These are updates to the Web's publishing language, HTML. HTML 4.0 lets you use cascading style sheets (CSSs) to place objects precisely on your Web pages. DHTML enables you to animate objects by moving them across the page.

So that you don't have to write code to use these features on your pages, Adobe GoLive offers built-in tools that make the creation process easier. For example, Adobe GoLive provides floating boxes that let you visually specify the position of any object.

In this part of the lesson, you'll create two floating boxes. You'll fill one with text and the other with an image.

1 Double-click the file Forever.html in the Pages folder in the site window to open the Web page.

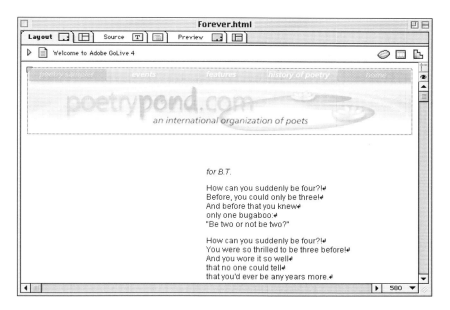

2 Click the Basic tab (▢) in the Palette.

Next, you'll place the anchor for the floating box between the banner graphic at the top of the page and the poem. To do so, you'll need to set the insertion point just past the banner graphic. The easiest way to do this is to move the pointer onto the right side of the banner graphic. Because GoLive can't place the anchor directly onto the banner graphic, the anchor will go to the next available place after the graphic.

3 Drag the Floating Box icon from the Palette to the right side of the banner graphic on the Web page.

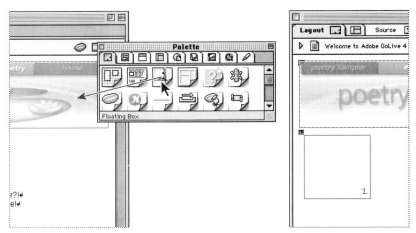

Dragging floating box icon and result

The Inspector changes to the Floating Box Inspector.

Text, images, JavaScript applets, and QuickTime movies can be placed inside a floating box. Here, you'll enter text into the floating box.

4 Click inside the floating box and type **Forever Four**, the title of the poem.

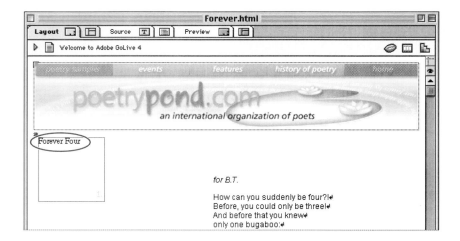

5 Drag to select the type.

6 In the toolbar, click the Bold button (B) and choose 6 from the Font Size menu (3 ⬍).

7 Choose Style > Font > Arial for the typeface.

8 Move the pointer over the floating box until the pointer changes to a hand pointing left; and then click to select the floating box.

In the Floating Box Inspector, enter **Title** for Name and click the Enter button in the Inspector or press Enter or Return. This names the floating box so it's easier to work with when you have multiple ones. (Whenever the Enter button appears after a text box or field, you must click the button or press Enter or Return on the keyboard to apply the value.)

You can resize the floating box so that the title fits on one line.

9 Move the mouse pointer to the bottom right corner of the floating box.

10 When the pointer changes to an arrow, drag the corner of the floating box so that both words in the title fit on the same line. Drag again to fit the floating box closely around the title.

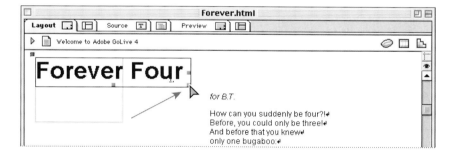

11 In the Floating Box Inspector, enter **135** for Left and press Enter or Return. Then enter **125** for Top and press Enter or Return to specify an exact location for the floating box.

You've finished making your first floating box.

12 Choose File > Save.

Adding one floating box on top of another

Now you'll add a second floating box. This one will contain an image.

 1 Drag the Floating Box icon from the Palette just to the right of the small yellow anchor of the first floating box. (You can tell you are dragging to the correct location when a blinking vertical cursor appears to the right of the first floating box's anchor. The resulting floating box should appear as shown in the illustration.)

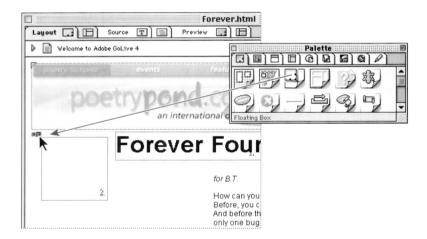

2 In the Floating Box Inspector, enter **Duck** for Name and press Enter or Return so you can differentiate it from the Title floating box you added earlier.

 3 Drag the Image icon from the Palette into the floating box you just made.

The image placeholder is now inside the floating box and the Inspector changes to the Image Inspector.

Now you'll connect the image placeholder to an image file.

4 Hold down Alt (Windows) or Command (Mac OS) and drag from the image place-holder on the Web page to the file Duck.gif in the Media folder in the site window. (This method has the same effect as dragging from the Point and Shoot button in the Image Inspector to a file in the site window.)

The image of a Duck appears in the floating box.

This time, rather than specifying values in the Floating Box Inspector, you'll drag the floating box to place it.

5 Click the side of the new floating box to select it. Make sure the floating box is selected and not just the image within it. You can tell the floating box is selected when the pointer changes to a hand pointed to the left. If the hand is pointed up, the image is selected, not the floating box.

6 Drag the new floating box so its right side is against the left edge of the poem and its top is lined up with the title "Forever Four." The duck is now blocking part of the title.

7 Choose File > Save.

Notice that you didn't use a layout grid on this page to locate objects precisely. That's because floating boxes enable you to move objects around without the need for tables or layout grids. In fact, as more people design and view pages using HTML 4.0-compliant applications, the need to use tables to position items may disappear.

Changing the stacking order

You can change the order in which floating boxes are stacked on top of each other. Here, you'll change the stacking order so that the floating box containing the title is on top of the floating box with the duck image.

The stacking order is initially determined by the location of the anchor on the page. That is, the further down and to the right a floating box's anchor is compared to others on the page, the higher in the stack it is. However, specifying a depth in the Floating Box Inspector overrides the default stacking order. The number that appears in the bottom right corner of the floating box indicates the order in which that floating box was added to the page.

1 Select the floating box containing the duck. (Remember, the floating box is selected when the hand points to the left.)

2 In the Floating Box Inspector, enter **1** for Depth and press Enter or Return.

3 Select the right side of the floating box containing the title "Forever Four" (where it isn't under the other floating box).

4 In the Floating Box Inspector, enter **2** for Depth and press Enter or Return.

Because the floating box with the title has a higher number, it moves on top.

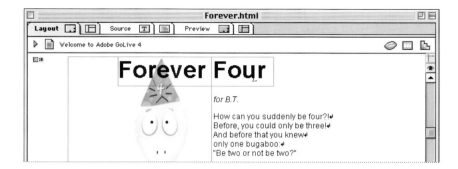

5 Choose File > Save.

6 Close the page Forever.html.

Animating floating boxes

In this part of the lesson, you'll learn how to animate floating boxes so they move across the page.

1 Double-click the file Night.html in the Pages folder in the site window to open the Web page.

This page contains a floating box with an image of musical notes in it.

2 Click the TimeLine Editor button ( ) at the top right of the document window.

The TimeLine Editor appears. In the tour, you animated a floating box by dragging it around. Here, you'll animate a floating box using the Timeline Editor window for much greater accuracy and control of the animation.

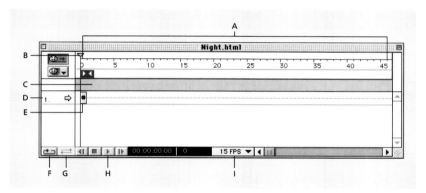

A. Frame markers ***B.*** *Time Indicator* ***C.*** *Action Track* ***D.*** *Time Track for floating box*
E. *First keyframe* ***F.*** *Loop button* ***G.*** *Palindrome ("back and forth") button*
H. *Play button* ***I.*** *Frames per second menu*

Using keyframes

Keyframes indicate particular points (called "frames") along the timeline of the animation. You add keyframes to the TimeLine Editor. Then you select a keyframe and move the floating box to a location on the Web page. As the animation runs and the time indicator reaches that keyframe, the floating box moves to the location on the Web page.

1 Select the floating box containing the musical notes. (Remember, the hand points to the left when the floating box is selected.)

2 Click the initial keyframe in the TimeLine to select it.

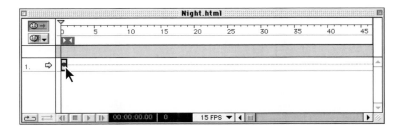

3 With the keyframe selected, drag the floating box just to the right of the nightingale's beak. This specifies where the floating box should be when the animation starts.

Note: *Throughout this lesson, in Windows, click once in the document window to select the window before dragging the floating box.*

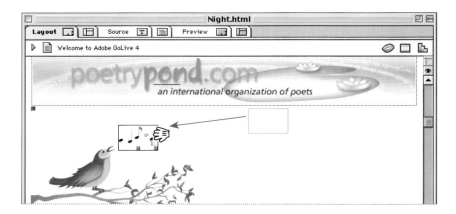

Now you'll add another keyframe and move the floating box to its next position in the animation.

4 Control-click (Windows) or Command-click (Mac OS) in the time track to add another keyframe at the 30 frame mark. (If you don't create the keyframe at the correct frame mark, you can drag it into position.)

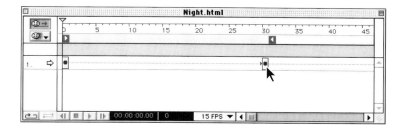

5 Select the keyframe. (If you don't, the previous keyframe remains selected, and the animation will move back and forth when you play it.)

6 Drag the floating box to just below the bottom right corner of the banner.

Now you can play the animation.

7 Click the Play button (▶) near the bottom left of the TimeLine Editor. Usually, because you are already at the end of an animation, you'll need to click the Play button a second time to restart the animation from the beginning.

The animation plays one time and stops. Now you'll make it loop back and forth and change its speed.

8 Click the Loop button (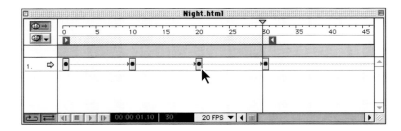) and Play button on the TimeLine Editor to see the animation repeat continually. Then click the Palindrome button ( ) on the TimeLine Editor to see the animation loop forwards and backwards.

9 Choose different speeds from the FPS (Frames Per Second) menu at the bottom of the timeline to see the animation move faster and slower.

10 When you're through experimenting, choose 20 FPS from the Frames Per Second menu.

11 Click the Stop button ( ) to stop the animation.

12 Choose File > Save.

Editing keyframes

1 Control-click (Windows) or Command-click (Mac OS) to add another two keyframes between the two existing ones, one at the 10 frame mark and the other at the 20 frame mark.

2 Select the keyframe at the 10 frame mark and drag the floating box to a spot just below the middle of the banner. (Remember, the hand must be pointing to the left to select the floating box.)

3 Select the keyframe at the 20 frame mark and drag the floating box to a location above the title.

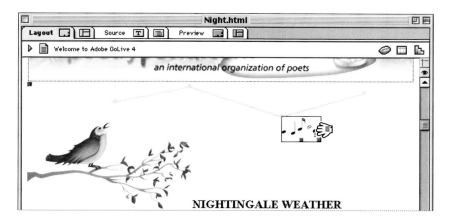

4 Click the Play button (▶) to play the animation again.

5 Click the Stop button (■) to stop the animation.

Rather than have the floating box move in sharp angles from keyframe to keyframe, you'll smooth out the animation path.

6 Shift-click each keyframe or drag from the side or below to select all four keyframes. You can only change the animation path by selecting one or more keyframes first and making sure the time indicator is at one of the keyframes.

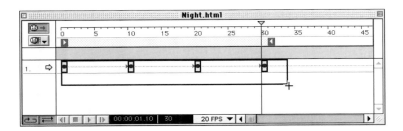

7 In the Animation area of the Floating Box Inspector, choose Curve from the Type menu.

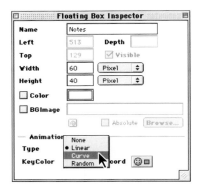

8 Play the animation. Notice how much smoother the motion is now.

9 Stop the animation.

10 Choose File > Save.

11 Experiment with adding some keyframes (remember to then select the keyframe and move the floating box to a new position) and deleting others (by selecting a keyframe and pressing Delete). Then play and stop the animation.

12 Close the TimeLine Editor and the Night.html Web page when you're done. Don't save the Web page again, since you don't want to keep the experimental animation you just did in the previous step.

Animating multiple floating boxes

Now that you've animated a single floating box, you're ready to animate multiple floating boxes.

1 Double-click the file Haiku.html in the Pages folder in the site window to open the Web page.

This page already contains the following objects:

• A large floating box named Poem with an image of a poem, pond, and reeds in it.

• An animated floating box named Jumper with an image of a jumping frog in it.

• A floating box named Dragonfly with an image of a dragonfly in it.

In this part of the lesson, you'll animate the Dragonfly floating box so that it passes in front of and then behind the reeds.

First, you'll use the Floating Box Controller to temporarily lock the other two floating boxes in place so you don't accidentally select or move them.

2 If necessary, choose View > Floating Box Controller (Windows) or Window > Floating Box Controller (Mac OS) to display the palette.

3 In the Floating Box Controller, click the Pencil icons next to Poem and Jumper so they are dimmed. The Poem and Jumper floating boxes are now locked in place for the current keyframe.

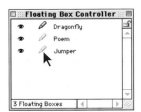

4 Click the TimeLine Editor button (▦) at the top right of the document window to display the TimeLine Editor.

Notice that the TimeLine Editor displays a separate track for each floating box on the page. This enables you to animate each floating box separately. The number in the bottom right corner of each floating box corresponds to the track numbers in the TimeLine Editor.

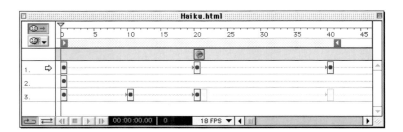

5 Select the Dragonfly floating box on the Web page. (Remember, the hand must be pointing left.)

The name Dragonfly is highlighted in the Floating Box Controller and an arrow appears next to its track (track 1) in the TimeLine Editor.

6 Click to select the first keyframe in track 1.

7 Drag the Dragonfly floating box to its initial position near the top center of the Poem floating box.

8 Ctrl-click (Windows) or Command-click (Mac OS) to create a second keyframe for the floating box at frame 20 in the TimeLine Editor.

9 Select the keyframe at frame 20 and drag the Dragonfly floating box down and to the right of the reeds.

Notice that when you select the keyframe at frame 20, the other floating boxes are shown in their positions at frame 20 as well.

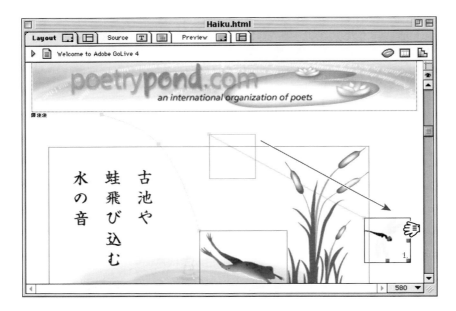

10 Ctrl-click/Command-click to create a third keyframe for the floating box at frame 40.

11 Select the keyframe and drag the floating box back to its starting position at the middle of the page.

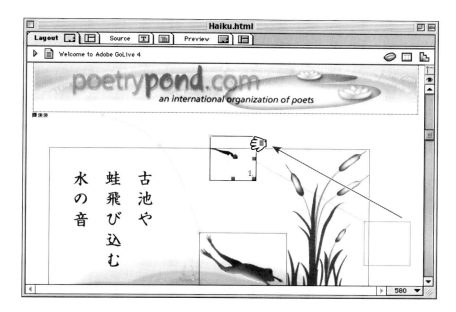

To get the floating box to the same starting position, you can select the first keyframe (at frame 0) and note the left and top coordinates in the Keyframe Inspector. Then select the keyframe at frame 40 and enter the coordinates from the keyframe at frame 0.

12 Play the animation.

The dragonfly goes back and forth in front of the reeds and the frog jumps into the pond. Now you'll make the dragonfly go behind the reeds as it passes them from right to left.

13 Stop the animation.

14 Click to select the first keyframe for track 2, which is the track of the floating box containing the reed.

15 In the Floating Box Inspector, enter **2** for Depth and press Enter or Return. This sets the depth of the Poem floating box (which contains the reeds) in the stacking order of floating boxes on the page. By giving it a depth of 2, you have room to give the Dragonfly floating box a higher and lower depth.

16 Click to select the first keyframe in the track of the Dragonfly floating box (it's in track 1). Then enter **3** for Depth in the Floating Box Inspector and press Enter or Return.

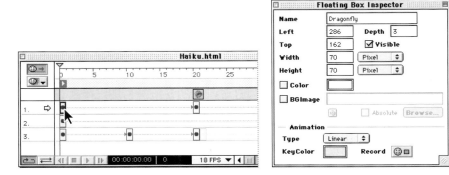

17 Select the second keyframe in that track, enter **1** for Depth, and press Enter or Return. The lower depth will put the Dragonfly floating box behind the reeds beginning at this keyframe.

18 Select the last keyframe for the track of the Dragonfly floating box, enter **3** for Depth, and press Enter or Return. This will return the Dragonfly floating box to be in front of the reeds in the stacking order.

19 Play the animation.

Notice that the dragonfly now seems to circle the reeds, first passing in front of and then passing behind them.

20 Stop the animation and choose File > Save.

21 Close the TimeLine Editor and close the Haiku.html file.

Actions

Actions are premade scripts that let you trigger events such as playing back animations, dynamically changing the content of images, and controlling different processes on the page. Actions can be attached to text, images, and floating boxes.

In this part of the lesson, you'll add an action to a rollover button, so that clicking the rollover button hides an animation. The animation, in turn, will have an action that causes a title to appear as it moves into place, and a second animation will have an action that causes a poem to appear line by line.

1 Double-click the file Prince.html in the Pages folder in the site window to open the page. Because you'll edit it, be sure that the page is in Layout view.

This page contains a rollover button of a frog to which you'll attach an action. (You may need to scroll down the page to see the frog.)

There are also two animated floating boxes on the page, one for the title for a poem, and the other for the poem itself. Currently, you can only see how the page looks during the first frame of the animation, in which the animated floating boxes aren't visible yet. As the animation runs, these floating boxes and their contents will appear and move into place.

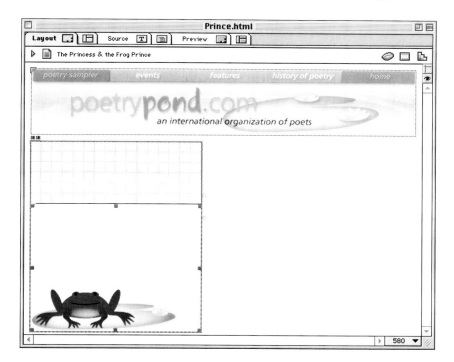

Adding an action to a page

Netscape Navigator contains a program error that causes Web pages to have trouble displaying animations when visitors resize the page. Here, you'll add an action that prevents this problem. It's a good idea to add this action to any page containing animated floating boxes.

1 Click the triangle next to the Page icon (📄) in the document window to display the head section pane.

Result of clicking the triangle

2 Click the CyberObjects tab (⊞) in the Palette.

3 Drag the Action Headitem icon from the Palette to the head section pane of the document window.

The Inspector changes to the Action Inspector.

4 In the Action Inspector, choose On Load from the Exec. (Execute) menu. Then choose Others > Netscape CSS Fix from the Action menu.

5 Click the triangle next to the Page icon in the document window to close the head section pane.

6 Choose File > Save.

Adding an action to a rollover

Now you'll add a trigger and action to the rollover button.

1 Select the image of the frog on the page.

Because the image is a rollover button, the Inspector changes to the Button Inspector.

2 Click the Actions tab in the Button Inspector.

3 Select Mouse Click listed under Events in the Button Inspector. This specifies an action to be triggered when a visitor to the Web page clicks the rollover.

4 Click the (+) button next to Actions in the Button Image Inspector. This adds the action to the list of actions.

Now you'll choose the action you want to occur. In this case, you'll link it to the animated floating box that contains the poem's title, "The Princess and the Frog Prince."

5 Choose Multimedia > ShowHide from the Action menu in the Button Inspector.

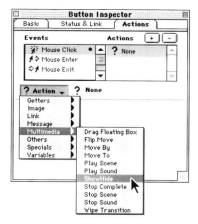

Notice that Show/Hide (NS 4, IE 4) appears next to the menu. This indicates that visitors to your page will need an HTML 4.0-compatible browser such as Netscape Navigator 4 or Internet Explorer 4 to view the animation.

6 From the Floating Box menu below the Action menu, choose Title. This indicates that you want the action to affect the floating box named Title. This is the floating box that contains the poem's title, "The Princess and the Frog Prince."

7 Choose Hide from the Mode menu. This will make the floating box containing the poem's title disappear when a visitor clicks the rollover button.

You've just added your first action.

8 Choose File > Save to save your work.

Adding actions to animations

You can add actions to animations as well.

1 Click the TimeLine Editor button (▦) at the top right of the document window to display the TimeLine Editor.

The TimeLine Editor contains two animation tracks, called *Time Tracks*. Track 1 controls the floating box that contains the poem's title and track 2 controls the floating box that contains the poem.

2 Click the Play button (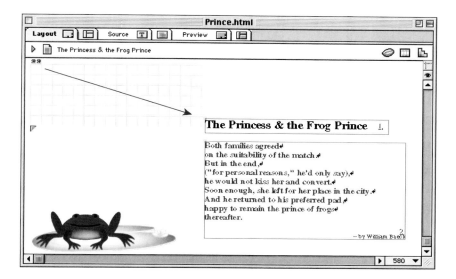) in the TimeLine Editor. Notice that at frame 10 of the animation the title suddenly appears and begins moving across the page. Then at frame 50, the text of the poem appears.

3 Use the scroll buttons at the bottom of the TimeLine Editor to scroll back to the first frames of the animation track.

Now you'll add an action to the animation track for the floating box with the title in it.

4 In track 1 of the TimeLine Editor, click to select the keyframe at frame 10. Notice that the floating box now displays the title. You'll add an action so that instead of the title becoming visible suddenly, it will gradually appear from left to right as it floats across the page.

5 Control-click (Windows) or Command-click (Mac OS) in the Action track (the gray track) in the TimeLine Editor, directly over the keyframe at frame 10.

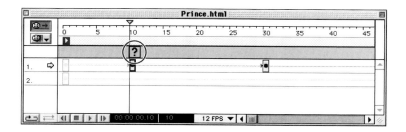

The Inspector changes to the Action Inspector.

6 Choose Multimedia > Wipe Transition from the Action menu in the Action Inspector.

7 Choose Title from the Floating Box menu to select that floating box.

8 Choose Wipe In From Left To Right from the Transition menu to specify the kind of transition you want. Then enter **30** in the Steps text box to make the transition occur in 30 steps. (More steps make the transition longer and smoother.)

9 Choose File > Save to save the page.

Finally, you'll add an action to the Time Track for the floating box with the poem in it.

10 Use the scroll buttons at the bottom of the TimeLine Editor to scroll to frame 50 of the animation track.

11 In track 2 of the TimeLine Editor, select the keyframe at frame 50.

The floating box now displays the poem as well as the title over it. You'll add an action so that instead of becoming visible suddenly, the poem will gradually appear line by line from top to bottom.

12 Control-click (Windows) or Command-click (Mac OS) in the Actions track in the TimeLine Editor, above the keyframe at frame 50.

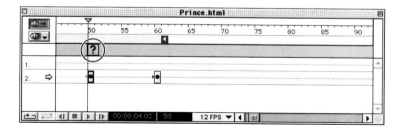

13 From the Action menu in the Action Inspector, choose Multimedia > Wipe Transition.

14 Choose Poem from the Floating Box menu to select that floating box.

15 Choose Wipe In From Top To Bottom from the Transition menu to specify the kind of transition you want. Then enter **15** in the Steps text box to make the transition occur slowly.

16 Choose File > Save to save the page.

17 Close the page.

You've just finished adding actions to the page!

Viewing the page

Because actions can't be previewed in Adobe GoLive, you'll view the finished page using your Web browser.

1 Start a Web browser that supports DHTML, such as Netscape Communicator™ 4.0 or Internet Explorer™ 4.0.

2 Use the Open or equivalent command in the browser to open the Prince.html file:

• In Windows, the path is Lesson05/05Start/Poetry Folder/Poetry/Pages/Prince.html.

• In Mac OS, the path is Lesson05/05Start/Poetry f /Poetry/Pages/Prince.html.

3 When the title has moved into place and the entire poem is displayed, click the frog to trigger the action you added to it.

4 Click the active links in the Web page and explore the site you've modified.

Review questions

1 What are two ways of creating animations?

2 What is a rollover?

3 Name two advantages of using floating boxes.

4 What determines the stacking order of floating boxes?

5 How do you drag a floating box?

6 What does the Floating Box Controller do?

Review answers

1 You can create animations quickly by using the Record button in the Floating Box Inspector and dragging a floating box to record the motions. For more control, you can use the TimeLine Editor.

2 A rollover is an image that changes depending on whether the mouse pointer is away from, over, or clicking it.

3 Floating boxes let you precisely position objects on Web pages and you can animate them. They also give you a way to format groups of objects such as blocks of text without using tables.

4 Initially, a floating box's stacking order is determined by its anchor's location on the page, with the top leftmost anchor indicating a floating box lowest in the stacking order, and so on down and across the page. You can change the stacking order by entering a depth in the Floating Box Inspector.

5 To drag a floating box, move the pointer over it until the hand is pointing to the left; then drag the box. Otherwise, you will just drag the object inside the floating box and not the floating box itself. In Windows, you may need to click once in the document window before you can get the pointer to change to a hand pointing left.

6 The Floating Box Controller lets you lock floating boxes in place. In animations, the floating boxes are locked only for the selected key frame.

Lesson 6

6 | Forms

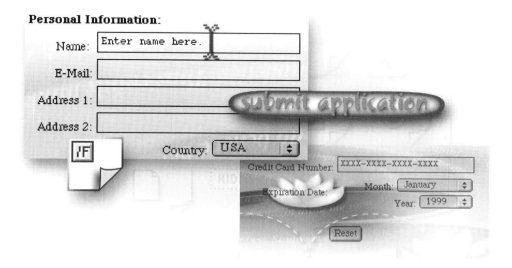

Forms are interactive elements that allow you to collect data from your site viewers. They enable viewers to request information or products, and to submit personal information, such as their name, address, and credit card number.

In this lesson, you'll learn how to do the following:

• Use a table to place form fields precisely on a page.

• Add a variety of form fields to a table, including text fields and a pop-up menu.

• Store frequently used objects in the Custom tab of the Palette, and add the objects to a page.

• Add radio buttons, a clickable image, and a Reset button to a form.

• Modify a list box in a form.

• Specify the order in which form fields are selected when viewers press the Tab key repeatedly.

This lesson will take about 45 minutes to complete.

If needed, remove the previous lesson folder from your hard drive and copy the Lesson06 folder onto it. As you work on this lesson, you'll overwrite the Start files. If you need to restore the Start files, copy them from the Adobe GoLive Classroom in a Book CD.

Getting started

In this lesson, you'll complete the design of a membership application form for a Web site called poetrypond.com. You'll create the section of the form that viewers will use to enter their personal information. You'll also add a variety of fields to existing sections of the form, including radio buttons, a clickable image, and a Reset button.

First you'll view the finished membership application form in your browser.

1 Start your Web browser.

2 Open the Index.html file to open the home page for the poetrypond.com Web site. In Windows, the path is Lesson06/06End/Forms Folder/Forms/Index.html. In Mac OS, the path is Lesson06/06End/Forms ƒ / Forms/Index.html.

3 Click the frog on the page to go to the membership application form.

The membership application form contains a variety of form fields, such as text fields for entering personal information, a list box for selecting poetry workshops, radio buttons for selecting a payment type, and a clickable image designed for submitting the application over the Web.

4 Try filling out the form by entering your personal information into the text fields and making selections from the list box, pop-up menus, and radio buttons.

The form has been designed for the purpose of this lesson only. Therefore, you won't actually be able to submit your application over the Web.

To submit and collect information from a form over the Web, you must have a Common Gateway Interface (CGI) application on a Web server to collect and route the data to a database. The names of the form fields must also match those set in the CGI application. Keep in mind that CGI scripts must be built outside of Adobe GoLive and require some knowledge of computer programming. CGI applications are usually set up by a Web server administrator.

5 When you have finished viewing the form, quit your browser.

About forms

The following illustration shows the finished layout of the membership application form in Adobe GoLive.

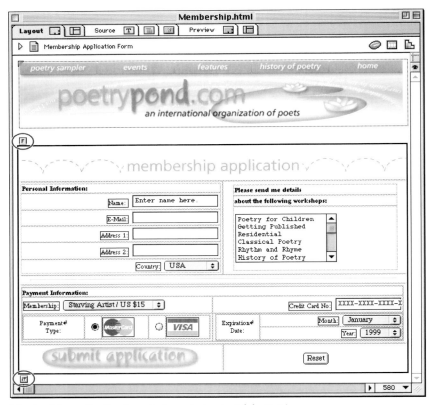

Membership application form in Layout view in Adobe GoLive

Notice that the form is laid out between two icons: a Form icon (🅵) and an End Form icon (🇮🇫). When you add these icons to a page, you are actually adding a Form and EndForm tag to the HTML source code for the page. These tags identify a Web page or section of a Web page as a form, and instruct the browser where and how to return form information for processing. The presence of these tags is necessary for the form to display and function properly.

[?] For information on how to add a Form icon and End Form icon to a page, see "Setting up the Form and EndForm tags" in Chapter 10 of the *Adobe GoLive 4.0 User Guide*.

Notice also that the form appears to be laid out on the page using one or more tables. The form is actually laid out using a table with two columns and five rows, and some of the cells in the table contain nested tables. You can use tables to precisely place form fields on a page.

The following describes the contents of each row in the main table:

• The first row of the main table contains the membership application image, which spans both columns.

• The second row contains two cells, each containing a nested table. The nested table in the first cell contains text fields for entering personal information. The nested table in the second cell contains text and a list box for selecting poetry workshops.

• The third row contains a line spanning both columns.

• The fourth row contains a nested table for entering payment information. This nested table actually contains two more nested tables, one for entering a membership type and payment type, and one for entering a credit card number and expiration date.

• The fifth row contains two cells, one with a clickable image designed for submitting the application over the Web and one with a Reset button.

Creating a section of a form

To get you started with the design of the membership application form, we've already created several sections of the form for you. You'll create the section of the form that viewers will use to enter their personal information. To do this, you'll use a new page. Later in this lesson, you'll add the contents of the page to the existing form.

1 Start Adobe GoLive. A new document named Untitled.html opens.

If you didn't start Adobe GoLive for the first time, a new document named Untitled.html may not be open on your desktop. If necessary, choose File > New to create a new page.

2 Choose File > Save As, rename the page **Name_form.html**, and save it in the Forms folder. In Windows, the path is Lesson06/06Start/Forms Folder/Forms. In Mac OS, the path is Lesson06/06Start/Forms *f* /Forms.

3 Select the page title, "Welcome to Adobe GoLive 4."

4 Type **Personal Information** as the new title, and click in the blank space beneath the title to deselect it.

Adding a table for the form layout

Now you'll add a table to the page. You'll use the table to place form fields precisely on the page.

We recommend that you always lay out a form using one or more tables. As an alternative, you can place form fields on a layout grid on the page. However, we don't recommend this technique because the layout of a form created with a layout grid can vary depending on the viewer's browser and screen resolution.

1 If necessary, choose View > Palette (Windows) or Window > Palette (Mac OS) to display the Palette, and make sure that the Basic tab ( ) is selected.

2 If necessary, choose View > Inspector (Windows) or Window > Inspector (Mac OS) to display the Inspector.

3 Drag a Table icon from the Palette to the page. The Inspector changes to the Table Inspector.

4 In the Table Inspector, enter **6** for Rows, and press Enter or Return. Enter **1** for Columns, and press Enter or Return. If necessary, choose Pixel from the Width pop-up menu. Enter **300** for Width, and press Enter or Return.

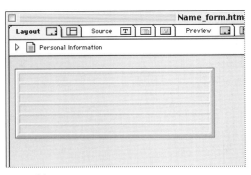

New table

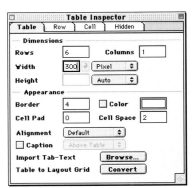

Setting table's properties in Table Inspector

Now you'll add a heading to the first cell of the table. This is the heading of the section of the form that you are creating.

5 In the document window, type **Personal Information:** in the first cell of the table.

6 Select the text you just entered, and choose Style > Structure > Strong to make the text bold.

7 Choose 2 from the Font Size menu (3) in the toolbar. By choosing a smaller relative font size, you can prevent the text from wrapping in the table cell when viewed in most browsers.

Remember that text appears larger in browsers for Windows. If you are designing your forms in Mac OS, you should keep your text small and leave extra space in your table cells. As a general rule, you should check your forms in browsers for both Windows and Mac OS before uploading them to a Web server.

8 Choose File > Save to save the page.

Adding a name field

Now you'll add a text field to the table that viewers will use to enter their name. When adding a text field, you'll also want to add a label. The label tells viewers what information should be entered into the field.

1 Click the Forms tab ( ) in the Palette. The Forms tab contains a variety of elements that you can add to a form, including the Form and End Form tags.

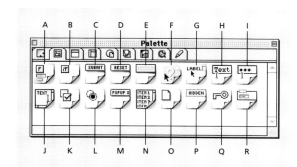

A. Form *B.* End Form *C.* Submit Button *D.* Reset Button
E. Button *F.* Input Image *G.* Label *H.* Text Field
I. Password *J.* Text Area *K.* Check Box *L.* Radio Button
M. Popup *N.* List Box *O.* File Browser *P.* Hidden
Q. Key Generator *R.* Fieldset

2 Drag a Label icon from the Palette to the second cell of the table.

3 Select the word Label. Then type **Name:** to change the label text.

💡 *To quickly select the label text, triple-click it.*

4 Select the text you just typed, and choose 2 from the Font Size menu (3 ⬍) in the toolbar.

Now you'll add the text field for the viewer's name.

5 Click after the label to insert a cursor. (Be sure to click after the label, not the label text.) Then press the spacebar to add a space.

6 Drag a Text Field icon from the Palette to the cursor on the page.

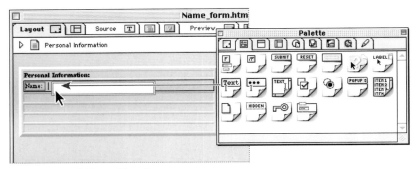

Dragging text field to table cell

The Inspector changes to the Form Text Field Inspector.

7 In the Form Text Field Inspector, enter **nameField** for Name. This names the text field.

8 For Value (Windows) or Content (Mac OS), enter: **Enter name here.**

The text you just entered appears in the text field on the page. When filling out the text field, viewers can replace the text with their own information.

💡 *If you prefer to design your form without the use of labels, you can simply enter information for the text field in the Value/Content text box instead.*

9 Enter **20** for Visible, and press Enter or Return. This is the number of characters that can be visible in the field.

10 Enter **40** for Max, and press Enter or Return. This is the maximum number of characters that can be entered into the field.

Adding address fields

Now you'll add three text fields to the table that viewers will use to enter their e-mail address and postal addresses. To save time, you'll begin by copying and pasting the label and text field from the second cell of the table to the third, fourth, and fifth cells.

1 In the document window, select the contents of the second cell in the table. (The second cell contains the Name label and the text field that contains the text "Enter name here.")

2 Ctrl-drag (Windows) or Option-drag (Mac OS) from the second cell down to the third cell. The contents of the second and third cell should now match.

3 Ctrl/Option-drag from the third cell down to the fourth cell. The contents of the third and fourth cells should now match.

4 Ctrl/Option-drag from the fourth cell down to the fifth cell. The contents of the fourth and fifth cells should now match.

5 Change the label text in the third cell to **E-Mail:**, change the label text in the fourth cell to **Address 1:**, and change the label text in the fifth cell to **Address 2:**.

6 Select the text field in the third cell with the "E-Mail:" label. (Be sure to select the text field, not the label.) In the Form Text Field Inspector, enter **emailField** for Name.

7 Delete the text in the Value/Content text box. Most viewers will understand what to enter in this field by following the example set by the name field. (Alternatively, you could edit the Value/Content field by replacing the word "name" with "e-mail address.")

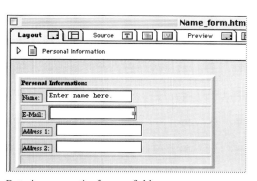 

Entering properties for text field

8 Select the text field in the fourth cell with the "Address 1:" label. In the Form Text Field Inspector, enter **address1Field** for Name. Delete or change the text in the Value/Content text box.

9 Select the text field in the fifth cell with the "Address 2:" label. In the Form Text Field Inspector, enter **address2Field** for Name. Delete or change the text in the Value/Content field.

Notice that every text field has an Is Password Field option in the Form Text Field Inspector. You select this option when you want a viewer to enter a password into the field.

Aligning table cells

Now you'll use the Table Inspector to align the contents of the table cells that contain text fields.

1 Move the pointer over the right or bottom edge of the second table cell until the pointer changes to an arrow. Click to select the cell.

The Inspector changes to the Table Inspector, with the Cell tab automatically selected.

2 Shift-click the right or bottom edges of the third, fourth, and fifth table cells to add them to the selection. All table cells that contain text fields should now be selected.

3 In the Table Inspector, choose Middle from the Vertical Alignment pop-up menu. Choose Right from the Horizontal Alignment pop-up menu.

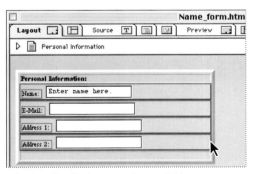

Selecting all cells that contain text fields

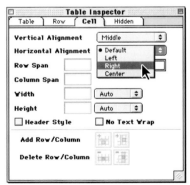

Selecting middle vertical and right horizontal alignment

4 Click in the blank space outside the table to deselect its table cells.

5 Choose File > Save to save the page.

Linking labels to text fields

Now you'll link each label to its corresponding text field on the page. By linking a label to a text field, you enable viewers to activate the text field by clicking its label. For example, viewers can click the "Name:" label to insert a cursor in the text box for entering their name.

First you'll link the "Name:" label to its corresponding text field.

1 Move the pointer to an edge of the "Name:" label, so that the pointer turns into a hand. Then click the label to select it. The Inspector changes to the Form Label Inspector.

2 In the Form Label Inspector, drag from the Point and Shoot button (回) to the text field that corresponds to the "Name:" label. The Reference text box in the Form Label Inspector displays a reference to the text field named nameField.

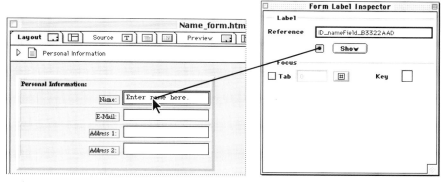

Linking label to text field

3 Select the "E-Mail:" label, and link it to its corresponding text field using the Point and Shoot button in the Form Label Inspector.

4 Link the "Address 1:" and "Address 2:" labels to their corresponding text fields.

Note: *If you copy and paste a label that has been linked to a form field, you need to relink the new label to the correct field. Otherwise, both labels will refer to the same field.*

5 Choose File > Save to save the page.

Creating a pop-up menu

Pop-up menus provides viewers with multiple options from which they can choose. Now you'll add a pop-up menu that viewers will use to choose the country in which they live.

1 Drag a Label icon from the Palette to the sixth cell of the table.

2 Select the word Label. Then type **Country:** to change the label text.

3 Select the text you just typed, and choose 2 from the Font Size menu ( ) in the toolbar.

4 Click after the label to insert a cursor. (Be sure to click after the label, not the label text.) Then press the spacebar to add a space.

5 Drag a Popup icon from the Palette to the cursor on the page. A placeholder for the pop-up menu appears on the page.

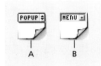

A. *Popup icon (Mac OS)*
B. *Popup icon (Windows)*

6 Move the pointer over the right or bottom edge of the sixth table cell until the pointer changes to an arrow. Click to select the cell.

The Inspector changes to the Table Inspector, with the Cell tab automatically selected.

7 In the Table Inspector, choose Middle from the Vertical Alignment pop-up menu. Choose Right from the Horizontal Alignment pop-up menu.

8 Select the pop-up menu placeholder on the page. The Inspector changes to the Form Popup Inspector.

9 In the Form Popup Inspector, enter **countryPopup** for Name. This names the pop-up menu.

You'll leave the Rows option at 1. This means that one row (or item) will be visible in the pop-up menu.

Now you'll use the Form Popup Inspector to add items to the pop-up menu.

10 In the Focus list box, click the first item to select it. (The first item is currently labeled "First" with a value of "one.")

11 In the first text box at the bottom of the Form Popup Inspector, enter **Canada** to replace the word "First," and press Enter or Return. In the second text box, enter **Country_Canada** to replace the word "one," and press Enter or Return.

The label "Canada" will appear as an item in the pop-up menu, and the value "Country_Canada" would be returned to the CGI script for the form when a viewer chooses this item.

12 Select the second item in the Focus list box. (The second item is currently labeled "Second" with a value of "two.") Use the text boxes at the bottom of the Form Popup Inspector to enter **France** as its label and **Country_France** as its value.

13 Select the third item in the Focus list box, and enter **Germany** as its label and **Country_Germany** as its value.

Now you'll add a fourth item to the pop-up menu.

14 To create a fourth item, click New. Then enter **USA** as its label and **Country_USA** as its value.

By default, the first item that you added to the pop-up menu (Canada) will display in the browser. However, because most potential viewers for this particular Web site will be from the United States, you'll change the default to display the USA.

15 In the Form Popup Inspector, click the check box next to the text box that contains the text "USA."

Specifying menu item that displays by default

The pop-up menu on the page now displays the text "USA."

16 Choose File > Save to save the page.

Setting table properties

You have finished adding the form fields to the table. Now you'll remove the border from the table and set other table properties. If you plan on removing the table's border in your forms, we recommend that you do it as a last step. It is easier to select table cells when the border is set at its default value of 4.

1 Move the pointer over the left or top edge of the table, so that the pointer turns into a hand. Then click the table to select it. The Inspector changes to the Table Inspector, with the Table tab automatically selected.

 You can use the Inspector to determine whether you have selected the table or a form field.

2 In the Table Inspector, enter **0** for Border, and press Enter or Return. Enter **2** for Cell Pad, and press Enter or Return. Enter **0** for Cell Space, and press Enter or Return.

3 Choose File > Save to save the page.

Using the Custom tab of the Palette to store and add objects

With Adobe GoLive, it's easy to copy and paste objects from one page to another. You can store frequently used objects in the Custom tab of the Palette, and then quickly add the objects to your pages.

Now you'll store the table that you've just created in the Custom tab of the Palette, so that you can quickly add it to the membership application form.

1 Click the Custom tab in the Palette ( ).

2 Click the left or top edge of the table on the page to select it.

3 Drag the selected table from the page to the Custom tab of the Palette. (Release the table when a thick black line appears around the tab panel.) An icon for the table appears in the Palette.

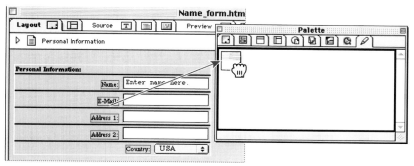

Dragging table from page to Custom tab of Palette

4 Double-click the table icon to display the Palette Item Editor. Then enter **Name and Address** for Item Name, and click OK. This names the table icon.

Objects in the Custom tab of the Palette are stored in your Adobe GoLive preferences. They can be added to pages in an existing site or a new site, and remain in the Palette until you clear or reinstall your preferences. You can delete an object from the Custom tab by clicking it to select it, and choosing Edit > Clear or pressing Delete.

Now you'll use the Custom tab of the Palette to add the table to the membership application form.

5 Choose File > Close to close the Name_form.html file.

6 Choose File > Open, and open the Membership.html file. In Windows, the path is Lesson06/06Start/Forms Folder/Forms/Membership.html. In Mac OS, the path is Lesson06/06Start/Forms *f*/Forms/Membership.html.

The membership application form opens.

7 Resize the Membership.html window to view as much of the form as possible. (To resize a window, drag its lower right corner.)

Notice that the form is missing several images and form fields.

8 Drag the table icon from the Palette to the table cell in the form that is directly below the words "Membership Application."

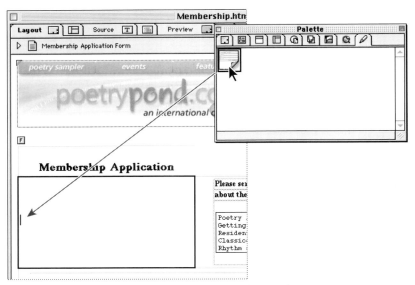

Dragging table icon from Palette to membership application form

The main table for the membership application form has been set up so that the Personal Information table fits properly in its designated table cell. Normally, you'll need to adjust the size of a cell in the main table, so that the nested table fits properly.

Before you begin creating a form, it's a good idea to carefully plan the its layout. You should decide on the contents of the main table, paying special attention to whether or not you will add nested tables to it. Careful planning will save you from having to redesign your form's layout during the creation process.

9 Choose File > Save to save the page.

Adding an image that spans two columns

Now you'll replace the words "Membership Application" by adding an image to the page. First you'll adjust the table columns so that the words "Membership Application" span across two columns.

1 Move your pointer over the cell that contains the words "Membership Application," so that the pointer changes to an arrow. Then click to select the cell.

The Inspector changes to the Table Inspector, with the Cell tab automatically selected.

2 In the Table Inspector, enter **2** for Column Span, and press Enter or Return.

Now you'll replace the text with an image.

3 Select the words "Membership Application," and press Delete.

You'll add the image to the form using a file in the site window.

4 Choose File > Open, and open the Forms.site (Windows) or Forms.π (Mac OS) file. In Windows, the path is Lesson06/06Start/Forms Folder/Forms.site. In Mac OS, the path is Lesson06/06Start/Forms ƒ/Forms.π.

The site window opens. It contains a Media folder, the Index.html file, and the Membership.html file. It also contains the Name_form.html file that you created earlier in this lesson; however, for this file to display in the site window, you need to update the contents of the window.

5 Click the Update button in the toolbar to update the contents of the site window.

6 In the site window, open the Media folder. Then drag Form_header.jpg from the Media folder in the site window to the empty table cell that previously contained the words "Membership Application." The image is added to the cell.

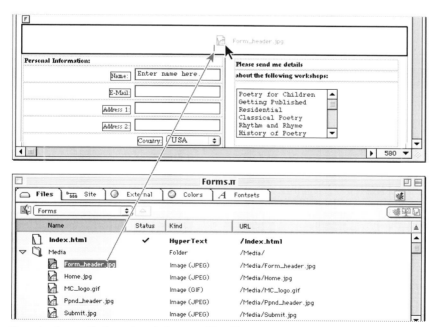

Dragging image file from site window to table cell

7 Choose File > Save to save the page.

Adding radio buttons

The Payment Information section in the lower right corner of the form already contains a nested table with one row and five columns that has been inserted into the main table. You'll add a group of radio buttons to this section so that viewers can select a payment type.

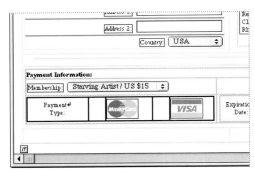

Payment Type section of form

If you created the Payment Type section from scratch, you would create it much in the same way as the Personal Information section. You would create a table with one row and five columns. Then, you would type the text "Payment Type:" in the first cell and insert images of a MasterCard and Visa card into the third and fifth cells. You would then add radio buttons to the second and fourth cells, as you are about to do in this lesson.

1 Click the Forms tab ( ) of the Palette. Then drag the Radio Button icon from the Palette to the empty table cell located to the left of the MasterCard image on the page.

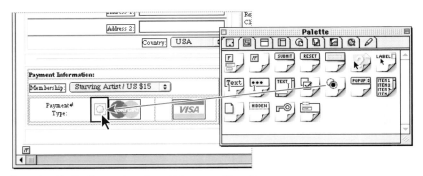

Dragging Radio Button icon from Palette to table cell

The Inspector changes to the Form Radio Button Inspector.

2 Drag another Radio Button icon from the Palette to the empty table cell located to the left of the VISA image on the page.

💡 *You can also copy the existing radio button on the page and paste it into the empty table cell. To do this, Ctrl-drag (Windows) or Option-drag (Mac OS) the radio button to the empty table cell.*

3 Click the first radio button that you added to the page to select it.

4 In the Form Radio Button Inspector, enter **paymentType** for Group. This names the group of radio buttons.

You'll use the same group name for the second radio button on the page. Using the same group name for the two radio buttons ensures that viewers can only select one option from the group.

5 Enter **mastercard** for Value. This is the value that would be returned to the CGI script for the form when a viewer chooses this option.

6 Select the Selected option. This makes MasterCard the preselected option.

Note: It's not required that you preselect any of the radio buttons.

7 Select the second radio button that you added to the page.

8 In the Form Radio Button Inspector, choose paymentType from the Group pop-up menu next to the text box. Enter **visa** for Value.

9 Choose File > Save to save the page.

Now you'll preview the page in Adobe GoLive to test the form fields that you've added to the page so far.

10 Click the Preview tab in the document window to preview the page in Adobe GoLive.

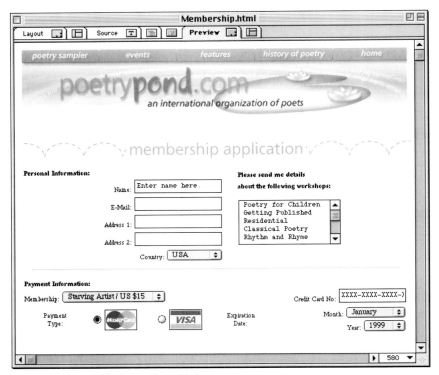

Previewing form fields that you've added to page

11 Try out the form fields that you've created by entering your name and addresses, choosing a country, and selecting a payment type.

12 Click the Layout tab in the document window to return to Layout view.

Modifying a list box

A list box in the upper right of the form provides viewers with a list of workshops from which they can choose. The list box was created much in the same way as the Country pop-up menu. You'll make several changes to the list box. First you'll specify for the list box to display six items rather than five.

1 Click the list box to select it. The Inspector changes to the Form List Box Inspector.

In the Form List Box Inspector, notice how the items for the list box have been entered in the same way as the Country pop-up menu. Each item has a specified label and value.

2 Enter **6** for Rows, and press Enter or Return. This will increase the rows (or items) visible in the list box to six.

Now you'll make the list box into a multiselection form field, so that users can select more than one workshop.

3 Select the Multiple Selection option.

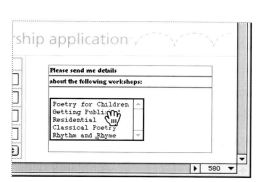

Selecting list box

Setting options in Form List Box Inspector

Now you'll add three more items to the list box.

4 Click New to create a new item. In the first text box at the bottom of the Form List Box Inspector, enter **History of Poetry**, and press Enter or Return. In the second text box, enter **Workshops_History**, and press Enter or Return.

5 If necessary, scroll down the Focus list box in the Form List Box Inspector to view the item you just added. (As an alternative, you can increase the size of the Inspector by dragging its lower right corner.)

6 Click New to create another new item, and enter **European Poetry** as its label and **Workshops_European** as its value.

7 Click New to create another new item, and enter **African Poetry** as its label and **Workshops_African** as its value.

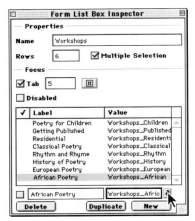

Creating additional labels and values in Focus list box

8 Choose File > Save to save the page.

Now you'll preview the page in Adobe GoLive to verify that the list box works as it should.

9 Click the Preview tab in the document window. To select more than one item in the list box, click the first item and then Shift-click to add additional items to your selection.

10 Click the Layout tab in the document window to return to the Layout view.

Adding a clickable image

Next, you'll add a clickable image to the form for submitting the application over the Web. This feature is one of the ways you can enable viewers to submit a form. An alternative way is to add a Submit button, which is discussed in "Adding a Reset button" on page 234.

1 If necessary, scroll down the Membership.html window to display the bottom of the form. The main table used to lay out the form has two empty cells in its last row.

2 Click below the MasterCard image to insert a cursor in the empty table cell on the left.

3 Drag an Input Image icon from the Palette to the cursor on the page. An Input Image placeholder is added to the table cell, and the Inspector changes to the Form Image Inspector.

4 If necessary, rearrange your desktop so that the image placeholder is visible in the document window and the Submit.jpg file is visible in the Media folder in the site window. Then click the Input Image placeholder on the page to reselect it.

5 Drag from the Point and Shoot button ( ) in the Form Image Inspector to Submit.jpg in the Media folder in the site window. The submit application image is added to the table cell.

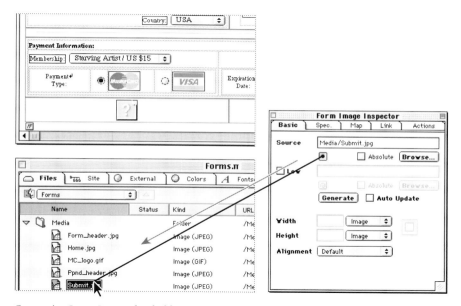

Connecting Input Image placeholder on page to image file in site window

6 Click the Spec. (Special) tab in the Form Image Inspector.

7 In Windows, deselect the Is Form option to activate the Alt Text box. The Inspector changes to the Image Inspector.

You'll only deselect the Is Form option temporarily in Windows. The Is Form option needs to be selected to specify the image as a clickable button.

8 In the Alt Text box, enter **Submit Image** as an alternative text message for the image, and press Enter or Return.

9 In Windows, reselect the Is Form option. The Inspector changes to the Form Image Inspector.

10 Enter **submitImage** for Name, and press Enter or Return. This names the clickable image.

11 Choose File > Save to save the page.

Adding a Reset button

You can add buttons to your form in at least two ways. The first method is to create an image of a button and link it to one or more actions. The second method is to use the Submit or Reset button in the Forms tab of the Palette. The following describes what happens when the viewer clicks one of these premade buttons:

• The Submit button sends a viewer's information to your database and closes the form.

• The Reset button deletes all of the viewer's information and returns the form to its default settings.

Now you'll add a Reset button to the form.

 1 Drag a Reset Button icon from the Palette to the empty table cell to the right of the submit application image. The Inspector changes to the Form Button Inspector.

The necessary options for the Reset button are preset. You only enter a name and label if you want to create a Normal button.

For more information about creating a Normal button, see "Using universal buttons" in Chapter 10 of the *Adobe GoLive 4.0 User Guide*.

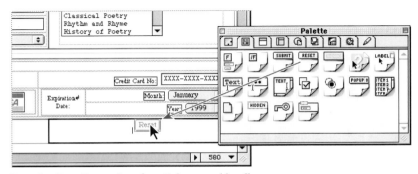

Dragging Reset Button icon from Palette to table cell

2 Choose File > Save to save the page.

Changing the main table's border and cell spacing

Now that you have finished adding images and form fields to the form, you can remove the border of the main table and the cell space of its table cells. (Both the border and cell space are currently set at 2, which has made it easier for you to select the table and its cells while modifying the form.)

1 In the document window, click the left or top edge of the main table to select it. The Inspector changes to the Table Inspector, with the Table tab automatically selected.

2 In the Table Inspector, enter **0** for Border, and press Enter or Return. Enter **0** for Cell Space, and press Enter or Return.

3 Choose File > Save to save the page.

4 Click the Preview tab in the document window, and check how the page appears in Preview view.

5 Click the Layout tab in the document window to return to Layout view.

Creating a tabbing chain

Now you'll add a navigational aid to your form—a tabbing chain that allows viewers to use the Tab key to move between form fields. To create a tabbing chain, you specify the order in which the form fields are selected by the Tab key. Adding a tabbing chain should be the last thing that you do to your form, after you are satisfied with the layout of your form.

Note: Some Web browsers will automatically allow users to use the Tab key to move between text fields. In addition, some browsers only allow users to use the Tab key to move between text fields and not other types of form fields.

You can start your tabbing chain with any form field. You'll start the tabbing chain for this form with the text field for entering a name.

1 Select the text field on the page that contains the text "Enter name here." The Inspector changes to the Form Text Field Inspector.

2 In the Form Text Field Inspector, select the Tab option. Enter **1** in the Tab text box. This specifies the text field as the first form field in the tabbing chain.

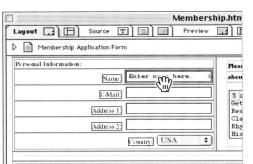

Selecting text field

Specifying text field as first in tabbing chain

3 Click the Start/Stop Indexing button (田). Yellow squares appear on each form field that can be part of the tabbing chain. (The yellow squares also appear on the form labels, although you can't add labels to your tabbing chain.)

The yellow square in the text field for entering a name already has a 1 in it, indicating that this field is the first in the tabbing chain.

Clicking Start/Stop Indexing button   *Result*

4 Click the text field for entering an e-mail address. A 2 appears in its yellow square.

5 Continue to create the tabbing chain by clicking on the yellow squares for the remaining form fields. (Be sure to click on the yellow squares for the form fields, not the labels.)

6 When you have finished creating the tab chain, click the Start/Stop Indexing button in the Inspector. The tabbing chain has been created, and the yellow squares disappear.

If you want to change the order of your tabbing chain, you can select each form field and enter a new number for it in the Tab text box of the Inspector.

▣ For more information about creating tabbing chains, see "Setting up tabbing chains" in Chapter 10 of the *Adobe GoLive 4.0 User Guide*.

7 Choose File > Save to save the page.

8 Click the Preview tab in the document window. Place your cursor in the text field for entering a name, and press Tab repeatedly to check that the tabbing chain works as it should.

9 Choose File > Close to close the Membership.html file.

Now you'll view the page in your browser.

10 Start your Web browser, and open the Membership.html file that you worked on in this lesson. In Windows, the path is Lesson06/06Start/Form Folder/Forms/ Membership.html. In Mac OS, the path is Lesson06/06Start/Form f/Forms/ Membership.html

11 When you have finished viewing the form, quit your browser.

In this lesson, you have learned how to lay out form fields using a table and how to add a variety of form fields to a form. Other form fields and functions that you can add to your forms include the following: check boxes, a file browser, a key generator, read-only and disabled form fields, bounding boxes with legends to group form fields, and hidden form fields.

▣ For complete information about creating forms in Adobe GoLive, see Chapter 10 of the *Adobe GoLive 4.0 User Guide*.

Review questions

1 What are form fields?

2 Why do you need to add Form and EndForm tags to each form?

3 Why should you avoid creating forms using a layout grid?

4 How can you add a clickable image to a form?

5 How do you add an item to a list box?

6 How do you create a tabbing chain for your form?

Review answers

1 Form fields are elements that you can add to your forms, such as text fields, radio buttons, or list boxes. Viewers can interact with form fields by entering information, clicking, or selecting items.

2 The Form and EndForm tags create the container for each form, and allow the form to display and function properly.

3 A form created using a layout grid can vary according to a viewer's browser and screen resolution.

4 To add a clickable image to a form, you can do one of the following:

• Drag an Input Image icon from the Palette to the form, and use the Point and Shoot button in the Input Image Inspector to connect the placeholder to an image file.

• Drag an Input Image icon from the Palette to the form, and use the Browse button in the Input Image Inspector to browse for an image file.

• Drag an image file directly to the input image placeholder in the form.

You should also make sure that the Is Form option is selected in the Input Image Inspector.

5 In the Form List Box Inspector, click New to create a new item. Then enter a label and value for the item.

6 To create a tabbing chain, select any form field in your form, and click the Start/Stop Indexing button in the Inspector. Click the yellow squares for the form fields (not the labels) in the order in which you want viewers to be able to select the form fields using the Tab key. Click the Start/Stop Indexing button in the Inspector to turn off the tabbing chain.

Lesson 7

7 Using Cascading Style Sheets

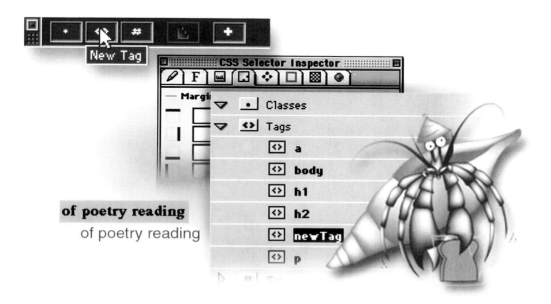

Using style sheets, you can easily update the style of large amounts of text and maintain consistency in typography and formatting throughout a site. Good, consistent design makes a site more inviting to viewers and easier to explore.

In this lesson, you'll learn how to:

• Identify styles applied to a document.

• Create styles that apply to HTML tags in a document.

• Create styles that apply to blocks of text.

• Create styles that apply to selected text only.

• Update styles and apply style changes globally.

• Duplicate and modify existing styles.

• Change the page color and margins using styles.

• Differentiate between internal and external style sheets.

• Link external style sheets to a document and use them to update a document's formatting.

This lesson takes about 1 hour to complete. If needed, remove the previous lesson folder from your hard drive and copy the Lesson07 folder onto it. As you work on this lesson, you'll overwrite the Start files. If you need to restore the Start files, copy them from the Adobe GoLive Classroom in a Book CD.

For information on setting up your work area, see ""Setting up your work area" on page 46.

Getting started

To see what you'll do in this lesson, first you'll view the final lesson file in your browser.

1 Start your browser.

2 Choose File > Open and open the Index.html file:

• In Windows, the path is Lesson07/07End/PoetryPond Folder/PoetryPond.com/ Index.html.

• In Mac OS, the path is Lesson07/07End/PoetryPond.com ƒ /PoetryPond.com/ Index.html.

3 Scroll through the page, and note its formatting.

4 Click the link "Benjamin Lucas." The formatting, including the links, all are controlled by a cascading style sheet.

5 When you have finished viewing the file, close it.

6 Close your browser.

About style sheets

HTML is a simple language that was intended to control the structure of information, not its presentation. Style sheets let Web designers enhance HTML's basic formatting by using styles to position text precisely, control type, and format elements on the page.

Cascading style sheets (CSS for short) are a simple way to add style to HTML documents and enhance the basic formatting of HTML tags. A style sheet is a set of stylistic rules that describe how HTML documents should appear to viewers. In HTML code, a *rule* is a statement about a stylistic aspect of one or more elements, in which a *selector* specifies what elements a *declaration*—consisting of a property and its value—will affect. For example, the style rule h1 { color : red } makes all head level 1s in a document appear red.

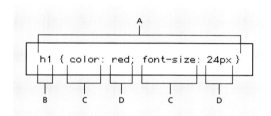

A. Rule B. Selector C. Property D. Value

In the past designers had to understand these concepts in-depth so they could write cascading style sheet code by hand in HTML. Now Adobe GoLive writes this code for you as you apply simple formatting commands much like in familiar word-processing or page layout applications.

In addition, styles are applied in a cascading fashion, from the most general to the most specific.

Adobe GoLive supports Level 1 Cascading Style Sheets (CSS1), which are part of the HTML 4.0 specification. Major Web browsers that support style sheets include Microsoft Internet Explorer 3, 4 and 5.0; Netscape Navigator 4.0; and Netscape Communicator 4.0. (Microsoft and Netscape browsers differ in what CSS features they support.) Web browsers must support CSS1 tags to be able to recognize and properly interpret style sheets.

A few considerations are key to using style sheets successfully:

• Stay current with what style sheet properties are supported by current browsers. The CSS1 specification is constantly evolving. Refer to www.w3.org/Style/ for the latest information.

• Experiment with applying different properties to different HTML elements. It's important always to preview the results in the current browsers to test your style sheet's effectiveness.

Exploring the style sheet tools

Three Adobe GoLive tools let you create and edit style sheets and link to external style sheets: the Style Sheet window, the Style Sheet toolbar, and the CSS Selector Inspector. This illustration shows the relationship between these three tools.

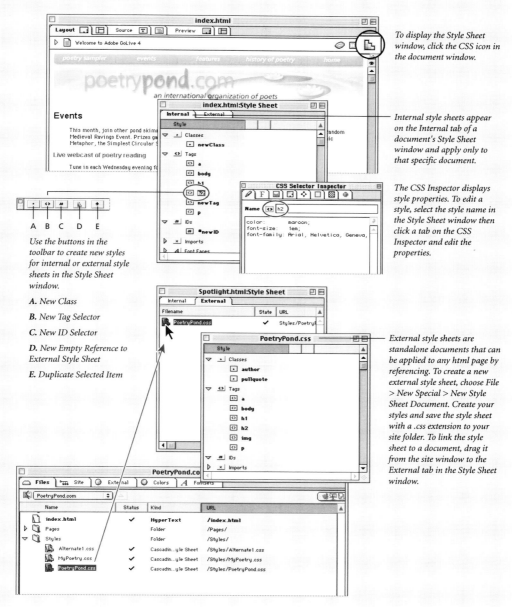

To display the Style Sheet window, click the CSS icon in the document window.

Internal style sheets appear on the Internal tab of a document's Style Sheet window and apply only to that specific document.

The CSS Inspector displays style properties. To edit a style, select the style name in the Style Sheet window then click a tab on the CSS Inspector and edit the properties.

Use the buttons in the toolbar to create new styles for internal or external style sheets in the Style Sheet window.

A. *New Class*

B. *New Tag Selector*

C. *New ID Selector*

D. *New Empty Reference to External Style Sheet*

E. *Duplicate Selected Item*

External style sheets are standalone documents that can be applied to any html page by referencing. To create a new external style sheet, choose File > New Special > New Style Sheet Document. Create your styles and save the style sheet with a .css extension to your site folder. To link the style sheet to a document, drag it from the site window to the External tab in the Style Sheet window.

Exploring an internal style sheet

You'll start your work in the lesson by exploring a style sheet that was created with a document.

1 Start Adobe GoLive.

2 Close the empty document that appears in the document window in Layout view.

3 Choose File > Open and open the PoetryPond.com site (Windows) or PoetryPond.com.π (Mac OS) file:

• In Windows, the path is Lesson07/07Start/PoetryPond.com Folder/PoetryPond.com.site.

• In Mac OS, the path is Lesson07/07Start/PoetryPond.com ƒ /PoetryPond.com.π.

As you work through this lesson, you'll overwrite the lesson files. Make sure that you keep a backup copy of the lesson Start and End files. If needed, you can copy the original lesson files from the Adobe GoLive Classroom in a Book CD.

4 In the site window, double-click Index.html to open the home page of the poetry site.

The basic structure and simple formatting of this document was achieved by applying the basic HTML tags such as <h1>, <h2>, and <p> to raw text. The finer styling such as the font size and color, margin widths, and even the white background of the document have been applied using a style sheet.

First, you'll view the document without the style sheet formatting.

5 Click the document window to make it active. On the right side of the document window, click the eye icon that appears beneath the CSS button. The Layout View Controller appears.

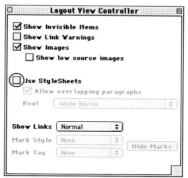

Clicking eye icon

Use StyleSheets option deselected in Layout View Controller

6 In the Layout View Controller, deselect the Use StyleSheets option. In the document window, notice how the document display changes when the style sheet isn't used.

In this example, the headings lose their color properties, the fonts change to a larger serif face, and the background of the entire document reverts to the standard gray of a basic HTML page.

Style sheet active

Style sheet turned off

You can see how the document got this basic HTML structure by checking the Format menu.

7 In the document window, insert the text cursor in the "Live webcast of poetry reading" heading, and then choose Format from the main menu.

The checkmark next to Header 2 indicates that the text is tagged as an HTML <h2>. Similarly the "Events" text is formatted as a Header 1, which translates to an HTML tag of <h1>; the body paragraphs are formatted as None, which translates to an HTML tag of <p>.

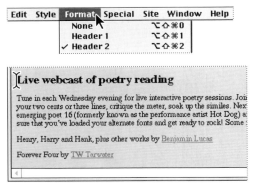

Header 2 format and corresponding text in document

8 If you're new to HTML, click the Source tab ([T]) in the document window to see how Adobe GoLive has written the HTML code and tagged the various chunks of text.

9 Click the Layout tab ([▣]) to return to the layout view of the document.

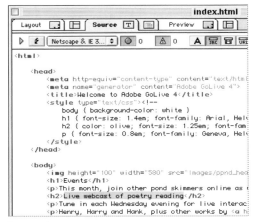

Source view

Now you'll take a look at the formatting that the style sheet controls.

10 Redisplay the Layout View Controller by clicking the eye icon ( ) on the right side of the document window. Select the Use StyleSheets option again to turn on the style sheet. The document window now displays formatting with styles.

Using the Root menu in the Layout View Controller, you can choose any of the popular browsers and see how the visual presentation changes. However, previewing with the Layout View Controller only simulates how the pages will appear in a browser, and is not a substitute for previewing how pages appear in an actual browser.

11 To view the style sheet, click the CSS button in the upper right corner of the document window ( ). This opens the Index.html Style Sheet window.

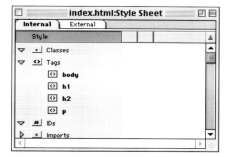

The Internal tab in the style sheet displays the different style sheet selectors that Adobe GoLive supports. These selectors include Classes, Tags, IDs, Imports, and Font Faces. (If the individual selectors don't appear, click the icon next to Tags to expand the list.)

• Tags are perhaps the most flexible selectors: they let you reformat the visible part of an HTML document based on its structure. The designer can define a style for any HTML tag, and it is applied automatically to all instances of the HTML tag throughout a document. Tag-based styles are fully compatible with browsers that can't read CSS1 information. So viewers with older browsers that don't support style sheets see the tag's plain HTML formatting, while viewers with newer browsers that support style sheets see the enhanced formatting. Tag selectors are also useful for ensuring that your documents will be readable in alternative browsers or on nonstandard viewing devices, such as a handheld PDA.

• Class selectors apply style formatting to specific instances of a text block, rather than all instances that share a common HTML tag. Unlike tags, class selectors are independent of the document's structure; they are defined by the designer but must be manually applied. Classes are useful for creating distinctive formatting like warning notes or pull quotes that you want to stand out from the rest of your text, or for creating special effects such as varying font sizes or colors within a word. However, don't use classes to structure a document visually; the formatting won't stick if viewers have non-CSS-compatible browsers. Instead, use tag selectors to achieve as much styling as you can and reserve class selectors for special (but not imperative) styling, at least until browser support for cascading style sheets improves and you are sure that most of your viewers are using the latest browsers.

• ID selectors let you embed a specific style for a unique paragraph or range of text in your document, and create unique type treatments. ID selectors also let you set properties for a floating box, and control its width, visibility, and absolute position. Applying an ID selector in Adobe GoLive requires that you edit HTML code.

• Imports and Font Faces display the import notations and font faces (if any) that Adobe GoLive finds when reading an existing document. These items are read-only and cannot be edited.

ID, Import, and Font Faces selectors are not covered in this lesson, but you can find more information on them in the *Adobe GoLive 4.0 User Guide*.

12 Notice that the Internal tab in the Index.html Style Sheet already lists some common HTML tags.

13 If the Inspector is not already open, choose View > Inspector (Windows) or Window > Inspector (Mac OS) to display it.

14 In the Index.html Style Sheet window, click a tag selector to select it. The CSS Selector Inspector becomes active.

15 Make sure that the Basic tab (✐) in the CSS Selector Inspector is selected.

16 In the Style Sheet window, click different tags. In the Basic tab in the CSS Selector Inspector, notice that the styles with their associated selectors, properties, and values appear.

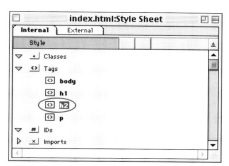

Tag selector selected in Style Sheet window

Style rules displayed in CSS Selector Inspector

Updating a style throughout a document

Now you'll edit a style to see how your document updates instantly.

1 If necessary, resize the document window so that you can see several different headings and body text.

2 In the Index.html Style Sheet window, select the h2 tag. Notice its attributes displayed in the Basic tab in the CSS Selector Inspector.

3 In the CSS Selector Inspector, click the Fonts tab (**F**). Choose a different color from the color pop-up menu (we chose Maroon), and see how the change is immediately reflected in the document window.

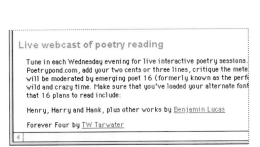

Different color applied to h2 tag

It's that easy to change a style that you've defined and apply it globally.

4 To make the font size a little smaller, enter **1.0** in the size field and choose em from the pop-up menu; then click the Enter button or press Enter or Return.

(Whenever the Enter button appears after a text box or field, you must click the button or press Enter or Return on the keyboard to apply the value.)

Note the different units of measure in the size pop-up menu. Em is a good unit of measure to use in style sheets, as it is always relative to the browser's font size; 1em is equivalent to the point size of the font in use. For example, if the viewer's default font size for <body> were 14 points, 2 em would be 28 points.

Alternatively, you can use percentage units because they're also relative. Pixels, on the other hand, aren't always the best choice because they constrain text to a specific size, which can vary depending on the platform and monitor resolution.

When you create a style using the CSS Inspector, Adobe GoLive writes the HTML code for you. Now you'll take a look at that source code.

5 Click the Basic tab in the CSS Selector Inspector, and note the h2 tag's properties.

6 Now switch to Source view in the document window by clicking the Source tab above the window.

7 Notice the statement:

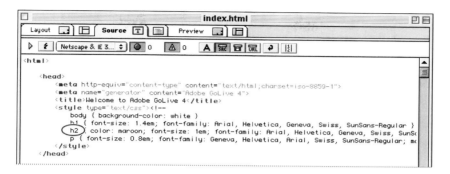

where h2 is the selector, and the information in brackets declares that the color property has a value of maroon, the font size property has a value of 1 em, and so on.

Remember that style rules are a statement consisting of a selector and a declaration on that element's property and value (that is, its specific appearance).

8 Click the Layout tab in the document window to return to Layout view.

Editing a style in a style sheet

You'll continue the lesson by editing another style in the internal style sheet. This time, you'll edit the style of the <p> tag to change the margins of the body text.

1 Click the CSS button ( ) in the upper right corner of the Index.html document window to redisplay the Index.html Style Sheet window.

2 In the Style Sheet window, click the icon to the left of Tags to expand the view; then select the <p> tag. Notice its attributes displayed in the Basic tab in the CSS Selector Inspector.

3 Click the Block tab ( ) in the CSS Selector Inspector. The right and left margins are currently set to 2%.

4 Enter **5** in the side margin text boxes, pressing Enter or Return after each entry, to indent the margins proportionally.

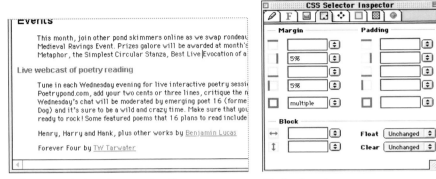

Side margins indented proportionally   Block tab settings

Notice how the left and right margins around all body text adjusts in the document window.

As you can see, properties can control the font, text (including the indentation, spacing, and alignment), box or document boundaries, positioning, border, background, and list (bullets and markers). Values specify measurements or colors.

Note: *Currently, all 4.0 browsers display only a few style properties including basic and some font properties. But browsers continue to add support for style sheet properties. For best results, test the properties you want to use in the latest versions of the most popular browsers. See "Previewing the results in current browsers" on page 267 for more information.*

Adding a style

Now you'll create a new tag-based style to alter the way the hypertext links appear throughout this document, removing the standard HTML underline, changing the color, and applying a boldface font. The standard HTML tag for formatting hypertext links is <a>. Whenever you create a hypertext link using the link command, Adobe GoLive automatically writes the source code for you, tagging the element as <a>.

1 To add a new style to the style sheet, click the New Tag button (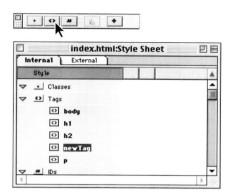) in the Style Sheet toolbar. A new item labeled newTag appears in the Style Sheet window under the Tag heading.

2 Click the Basic tab in the CSS Selector Inspector and name the style **a** to match the HTML link tag.

Whenever you create a tag selector, the tag names must match those of the HTML code. Style definitions don't use brackets, so don't include them as part of the name. The table "Common HTML tags" on page 256 lists common HTML tags and notes the Adobe GoLive commands used to apply them.

3 Press Enter or Return to create the tag.

4 Click the Fonts tab (**F**) in the CSS Selector Inspector.

5 Beneath the Decoration options, select None to remove the underline beneath hypertext. Notice that the underlines are removed from the existing links in the document.

Now you'll change the color of the hypertext font.

6 Choose a color from the Color pop-up menu and a weight from the Weight pop-up menu. (We chose Olive and a Bolder weight.)

Adobe GoLive features numerous ways to change the color of links. However, when you use a tag-based style to change the appearance of hypertext, you can then update all links on your site globally simply by editing the style. Later in this lesson, you'll use a similar technique to update the page's background color.

Note: *To delete a tag or class selector from a style sheet, select the item in the Style Sheet window; in Windows, choose Edit > Delete, and then click Yes; in Mac OS, choose Edit > Clear, and then click Remove.*

7 Choose File > Save to save the Index.html document. Saving this document also saves the internal style sheet.

8 Close the document.

Common HTML tags

Here are some common HTML tags you can use when creating tag-based styles in a cascading style sheet.

Element name	Abbreviation for	GoLive toolbar or menu command	Block or inline	Description
a	Link or anchor	New link	Inline	Highlighted
blockquote		Alignment commands	Block-level	Indented
body			Block-level	Inside canvas
br	Break	Shift + Return	Block-level	Breaks the line
em	Emphasis	Emphasis or Italic	Inline	Italic
h1, h2... h6	Heading levels	Header 1, Header 2, and so on	Block-level	Large fonts
i	Italic	Italic or Emphasis	Inline	Italic
img	Image		Inline	As an image
li	List item	Unnumbered list commands	Block-level	Bulleted list
ol	Ordered list	Numbered list commands	Block-level	Numbered list
p	Paragraph	Return	Inline	Regular text
strong		Strong or Boldface	Inline	Boldface

Creating a style sheet

Now that you've explored a style sheet, it's time to create your own from scratch.

Adobe GoLive supports two different kinds of style sheets: Internal and External. So far you have been working with a simple internal style sheet. Internal and External style sheets differ in how they work with Web pages. Internal style sheets apply only to the document in which they were created, and their styles cannot be exported for use with other documents.

Far more flexible than internal style sheets, external style sheets can apply to a group of documents or to an entire site. Rather than defining an internal style sheet for each and every page you want to apply some extra formatting to, it's easier to create a stand-alone external style sheet document. You can then refer to this external style sheet from any page to make its style options available.

1 Double-click the Spotlight.html file in the Pages folder in the site window to open the file.

2 In the document window, click the CSS button (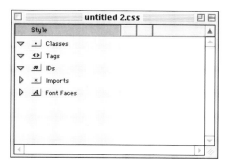) to display the Spotlight.html Style Sheet window.

Notice that no styles appear in the Internal tab in the Style Sheet window. The document has only the basic formatting from HTML tags; no styles are associated yet with any tags.

3 To create a new external style sheet, choose File > New Special > New Stylesheet Document to open an untitled .css window.

This window displays a list of selectors (Classes, Tags, IDs, Imports, and Font Faces) identical to what you saw earlier in the lesson on the Internal tab in the Style Sheet window. The only difference is that this style sheet is its own document, separate from the pages to which its styles apply.

4 If the Inspector is not open, choose View > Inspector (Windows) or Window > Inspector (Mac OS) to display it.

5 To add a new style to the style sheet, click the New Tag button in the Style Sheet toolbar. A new item appears in the Style Sheet window under the Tags heading.

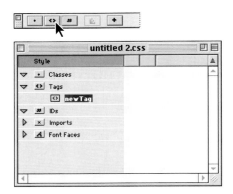

6 Click the Basic tab in the CSS Selector Inspector and name the style **h2**. Press Enter or Return to create the tag.

7 Click the Fonts tab (**F**) in the CSS Selector Inspector so that you can set font properties.

8 Click the New button, and use the pop-up menus to select a font color and font family. Choose a font size. (We chose Maroon, 1 em, and the sans serif group for font family.)

You've created the style, but nothing has changed in the document. In contrast with internal style sheets that instantly update their associated document, external style sheets must first be saved and attached to a document for the styles to be applied.

Saving and linking a style sheet

Now you'll save and link the style sheet to your HTML document. Once you link a style sheet to your document, Adobe GoLive applies its styles automatically.

1 Make sure that the untitled 2.css window is active. Then choose File > Save, and name the untitled .css document **MyPoetry.css**, and save it in the Styles folder within the PoetryPond.com folder.

It's important to use the .css extension so that browsers recognize the document as a style sheet. Saving the style sheet in a Styles folder is not mandatory but helps to keep your site organized and more manageable.

2 Click the CSS button ( ) in the upper right corner of the document window to display the Spotlight.html Style Sheet window if it isn't still visible. This window shows any internal and external style sheets that are associated with your HTML page.

3 In the Style Sheet window, click the External tab. As the palette shows, currently no external style sheets are linked to your page.

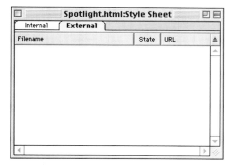

4 Make sure that the MyPoetry.css file in your PoetryPond.com site window is visible.

5 Drag the MyPoetry.css file from the site window to the External tab in the Spotlight.html Style Sheet window.

The second heading in your document (tagged h2) is reformatted automatically to reflect the style changes you specified in the previous procedure, and the External tab in the Style Sheet window is updated to reflect the linking of the MyPoetry.css document to your HTML page.

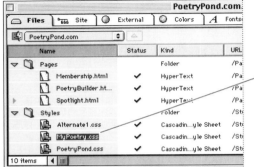

Style sheet applied (top); linking external style sheet by dragging it to External Style Sheet window (bottom)

It's that simple to create an external style sheet and link it to a document. Now you'll continue to refine the formatting of the Spotlight.html document by linking an additional style sheet to it. This style sheet already contains several styles to give you a jump start. You'll edit those styles and add some new ones.

6 In the site window, select the PoetryPond.css file in the Styles folder within the PoetryPond.com folder. This time, drag the style sheet to the Page icon (▤) of the Spotlight.html document window.

This is another technique for linking external style sheets to a document.

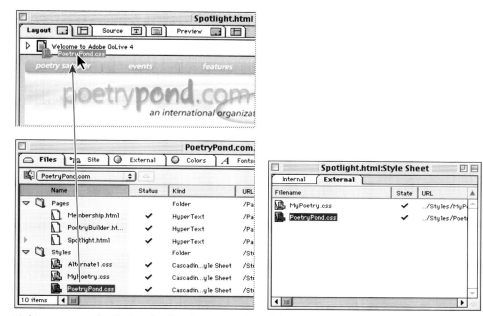

Linking to external style sheet by dragging to Page icon (left); updated External Style Sheet window (right)

Once again, the second heading (tagged h2) is reformatted, to reflect the properties in the style sheet you just attached. A feature of cascading style sheets is that you can attach more than one style sheet to a document and apply styles cumulatively or separately.

When a new style sheet uses the same style names as the previous one, the newer styles will take precedence and override the styles in the old style sheet. In this case, the h2 tag overrides that in the previous one (MyPoetry.css).

About cascading style sheets

A key feature of CSS is that they can cascade. That is, several different style sheets from different sources can be attached to a document, and all of them can influence the presentation of the document. For example, the default browser can attach a style sheet, a designer can have a style sheet to format a document, and viewers can add their own style sheets to address, for example, a larger font to compensate for poor eyesight or personal font preferences. In the case of conflicts, the CSS always chooses only one value, typically weighted first in favor of the designer, then the individual viewer, and then the default browser. (To override a designer's style rules, the viewer can turn off the designer's style sheet or mark certain style rules as "important.")

Creating a class style

Now you'll create a new class selector and apply its style to text in the Poetry page's Spotlight.html file. The first class you'll create will format a *pull quote*—some text or a quotation that is set off from the rest of the text for emphasis and for graphic impact.

1 In the External tab, double-click the PoetryPond.css to open the style sheet.

2 In the Style Sheet toolbar, click the New Class button (⊡) to create a new class. The Inspector changes to the CSS Selector Inspector.

3 In the Basic tab (✐) in the CSS Selector Inspector, name the class **pullquote**, and press Enter or Return.

4 Click the Fonts tab (**F**) in the CSS Selector Inspector, and use the pop-up menus and text boxes to set the pullquote's font properties. (We chose Olive, a font size of 0.75 em, and Italic style.)

5 Click the Block tab (⊡) in the CSS Selector Inspector, and set the left and right margins. (We used 15%.)

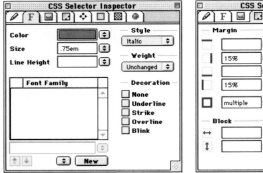

Fonts tab settings

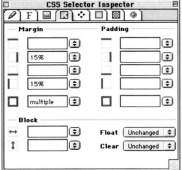

Block tab settings

Although you've created the class selector, it doesn't take effect until you apply it to a selection on the page.

Class selectors apply style formatting to specific instances of a text block, rather than all instances that share a common HTML tag. Unlike tag selectors, which are applied automatically to the corresponding HTML tag, class selectors must be explicitly applied to a selection.

6 In the document window, insert the text cursor in Lucas' sample poem. The Inspector changes to the Text Inspector.

7 Click the Style tab in the Text Inspector.

8 Click the Par column next to the pullquote class to apply that class to your selected text.

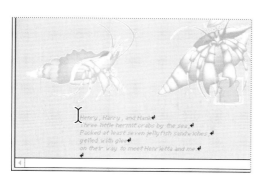

Text selection

Class applied to Par (paragraph) element

The Par option applies a style to an entire paragraph (or HTML block tag). In contrast, formatting an inline element applies the style only to the selection. See the table, "Common HTML tags" on page 256 for a list of block and inline HTML tags.

The Style tab also lists the Div element, which is a separate section of the HTML page, and the Area style, which applies a class to the entire body section of an HTML page. This lesson won't cover using these elements.

Duplicating a style

Now you'll create a new class for the author's attribution by copying the selector you just created.

1 In the PoetryPond.css Style Sheet window, select the pullquote class that you just created. You'll duplicate this class, and then modify its font to create a new class.

2 Click the Duplicate button (⊡) in the Style Sheet toolbar to duplicate the class selector. A new item called pullquote2 appears in both the Style Sheet window under the Classes heading and in the Basic tab in the CSS Selector Inspector.

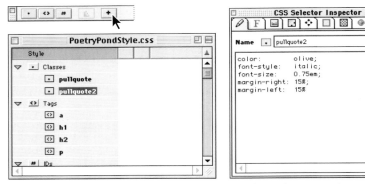

Duplicated class   *Duplicate class properties*

Now you'll edit the properties of this duplicate class.

3 In the Basic tab in the CSS Selector Inspector, rename the class **author** and press Enter or Return.

4 Click the Fonts tab (**F**) in the CSS Selector Inspector. Notice that the attributes for the pullquote class already appear. Change the font color to Black and the font style to Normal.

5 Click the Block tab in the CSS Selector Inspector, and enter a top margin of **–1**% to close up the space between it and the pullquote; then press Enter or Return.

Now you'll apply this new class style to your page.

6 In your document window, select the text "Benjamin Lucas" immediately below the pullquote.

7 In the Style tab in the Text Inspector, next to the author selector, click the Par column. This updates your page with this new format.

8 With the PoetryPond.css style sheet active, choose File > Save. Unlike with an internal style sheet that is attached to a document and considered part of it, an external style sheet is separate and any changes must be explicitly saved.

9 Make the Spotlight.html document window active, and choose File > Save to save your changes.

Changing the background color

Now you'll change the page's background color by using a style sheet. Adobe GoLive features numerous ways to change a page's background color. Doing it by using a style sheet is handy because you can change the backgrounds of all pages that use the style sheet with a single edit.

To apply a background color to your document using a style, you use a tag selector for the HTML body element. The body element contains all the displayed content of your HTML page.

1 View the body element by clicking the Source tab ([T]) in your document window. Look at what is contained between <body> and </body>.

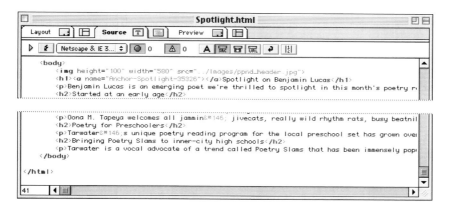

2 Click the Layout tab to return to Layout view.

3 Click the PoetryPond.css window to make it active. Then click the New Tag button on the Style Sheet toolbar. A new item appears in the Style Sheet window under the Tags heading.

4 In the Basic tab in the CSS Selector Inspector, name the item **body**, and press Enter or Return.

5 Click the Background tab (▨) in the CSS Selector Inspector, and choose White from the Color pop-up menu. The background of your document changes to white.

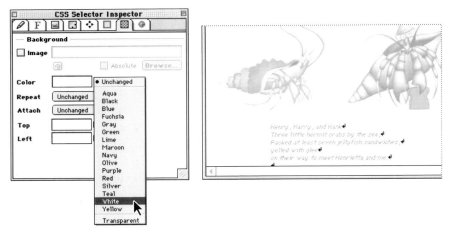

Selecting White background color   Result

You can also use the body element to change the color of the body text by selecting the body selector in the PoetryPond.css Style Sheet window, clicking the Fonts tab in the CSS Selector Inspector, and then choosing a color, and other properties.

If you like, try experimenting with other background colors. You can also try out different color combinations for the background and text font.

6 Choose File > Save to save changes to the PoetryPond.css style sheet.

As you saw with the h2 tag selector applied to the heading level 2, cascading style sheets first apply formatting generally, and then more specifically. The body tag controls the color of all text in the document, until another more specific style (for example, h1 or h2) specifies a different color for a more specific text selection.

Previewing the results in current browsers

It's a good idea to have the latest versions of both Netscape and Microsoft browsers installed on your computer system, so that you can preview how effectively and accurately your style sheets work in these different environments.

Web browsers must support CSS1 tags to be able to recognize and properly interpret style sheets. Currently, all 4.0 browsers display only a few style properties. Some properties work with a single browser only, some don't work at all but cause no harm, and others cause the browser to crash. For a list of browser-safe features, visit the Web Review's Style Sheets Reference Guide at www.webreview.com/guides/style/#charts.

1 If you haven't specified a preferred browser, choose Edit > Preferences, and click the Browser icon in the left pane of the Preferences dialog box. In the right pane, select a browser and then select the browser option next to the browser name (make sure that a check mark appears). Click OK.

If no browser is specified, you'll be prompted to select a browser to prevent the preview from displaying a blank page.

2 Click the Show in Browser button in the document window toolbar, or choose Special > Show in Browser to display the Spotlight.html document in your browser.

3 Notice how the different tag selectors (a, body, h2, and so on) and class selectors (pullquote and author) applied to the document appear in each browser.

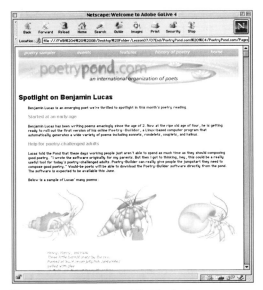
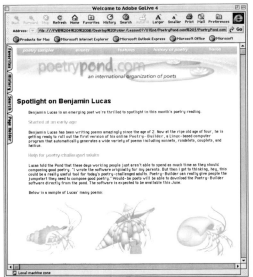

Netscape Communicator 4.0 style sheet preview   *Internet Explorer 4.5 style sheet preview*

4 For greater accuracy, launch your browser and then open the Spotlight.html document in your browser to preview the formatting.

Adobe GoLive simulates how a browser will apply the style sheet, but may not replicate the latest implementations of the style sheet standards.

If you launch more than one browser, check how each browser displays the different style selectors. (You should make sure that you have the latest version of the browser installed.)

5 Return to Adobe GoLive, and close the Spotlight.html document and its style sheets.

6 Close the PoetryPond.com site window.

This concludes the lesson. For additional practice using a style sheet, try the exercise in the next section, "Exploring on your own."

Exploring on your own

Cascading style sheets are easy to apply or to remove from your document. For additional practice, try out a style sheet that uses the same basic HTML tags, but has different style properties. When you apply the different style sheet to the same HTML document, you'll notice how easy it is to apply and change styles.

1 Choose File > Open and open the PoetryPond.com site (Windows) or PoetryPond.com.π (Mac OS) file:

• In Windows, the path is Lesson07/07Start/PoetryPond.com Folder/PoetryPond.com.site.

• In Mac OS, the path is Lesson07/07Start/PoetryPond.com ƒ /PoetryPond.com.π.

2 In the site window, double-click Spotlight.html in the Pages folder to open the document. You'll add an external style sheet reference to this document.

3 Click the CSS button in the upper right corner of the document window (⬚) to open the Style Sheet window.

4 Click the External tab in the Style Sheet window.

5 Click the New StyleSheet File (Windows) or the New Item (Mac OS) button (⬚) in the Style Sheet toolbar. A new item appears as "(Empty Reference!)" in the External tab in the Style Sheet window, and the Inspector changes to the External Style Sheet Inspector.

6 From the External Style Sheet Inspector, link the Alternate1.css file to the Spotlight.html document using either technique:

• Drag from the Point and Shoot button to the Alternate1.css file in the Styles folder in the site window.

• Click Browse, use the directory and folder controls to locate the Alternate1.css file in the PoetryPond.com/Styles folder, and click Open.

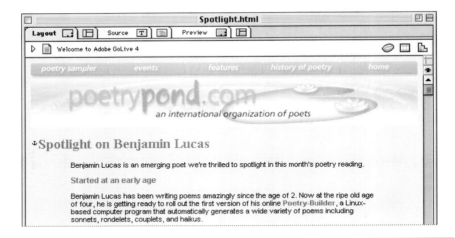

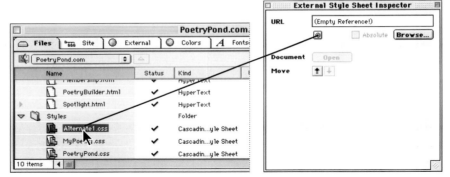

Alternate1.css style sheet applied (top); linking external style sheet from Point and Shoot button (bottom)

7 Notice how this style sheet reformats the document.

8 Close the PoetryPond.com site window.

9 Close the Spotlight.html document without saving your changes.

Review questions

1 How do styles differ from basic HTML formatting?

2 What does "cascading" mean when used to describe style sheets?

3 Why would a browser not display styles applied to a document?

4 How can you ensure that your style sheets work on the widest range of browsers?

5 What tools do you use in Adobe GoLive to create a style sheet?

6 What is the difference between an internal style sheet and an external style sheet?

7 What is the difference between a class selector and a tag selector?

8 What's the advantage of using a style to set the color of hypertext or the page background?

Review answers

1 HTML controls the structure of information (for example, different relative headings), but not its presentation. Style sheets let Web designers enhance HTML's formatting with precise positioning of text, control over type, and formatting of other elements on the page. For example, style sheets can be used to apply font size and color, margin widths, and even the background color to a document.

2 One or more cascading style sheets (CSS) can be attached to a document to influence the document's presentation. For example, a browser, then a designer, and then the individual viewer can all attach style sheets to a document. The influence of several style sheets "cascades" so that only one value is applied, typically that from the designer's style sheet. Styles within a style sheet also cascade, and apply progressively to a document. In addition, if a document uses multiple style sheets, the latest style sheet can override previously applied style sheets if they share the same tags; or it can enhance previously applied style sheets.

3 A Web browser must support CSS1 tags to be able to recognize and properly interpret style sheets. Currently, all 4.0 browsers display only a few style properties, and the browsers vary in which properties they support.

4 To use style sheets successfully, it's important to stay current with what style sheet properties are supported by current browsers; to experiment with applying different properties to different HTML elements; and always to preview the results in the current browsers to test your style sheet's effectiveness.

5 Three Adobe GoLive tools let you create and edit style sheets and link to external style sheets: the Style Sheet window, the Style Sheet toolbar, and the CSS Selector Inspector.

6 Internal style sheets are part of a document, are saved with it, and cannot be exported. They must be defined individually for each page to which their formatting will apply. External style sheets can apply to a group of documents or to an entire site. You can then refer to this external style sheet from any page to make its style options available.

7 Tag selectors are applied automatically by Adobe GoLive to their corresponding HTML tags and are fully compatible with browsers that can't read CSS1 information. Perhaps the most flexible selectors, tags let you reformat the visible part of an HTML document based on its structure. Class selectors apply style formatting to specific instances of a text block, rather than all instances that share a common HTML tag. Unlike tags, class selectors are independent of the document's structure; they are defined by the designer but must be manually applied.

8 When you set the color or attributes of hypertext or the page background using a style sheet, you can then change the hypertext or backgrounds of all pages that use that style sheet with a single edit.

Lesson 8

8 | Site Management

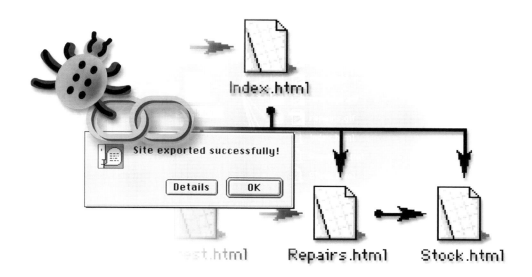

You can use Adobe GoLive's powerful site management tools to create and manage your site. These tools include the site window, which shows all the objects in your site, and the Site view, which is a hierarchical viewer and designer. Other management tools allow you to manage folders, files, links, and to import sites into Adobe GoLive, or to upload your site to a Web server.

In this lesson, you'll learn how to do the following:

- Look at a well-managed site.
- Import an existing non-Adobe GoLive site into the Adobe GoLive format.
- Explore the site window.
- Correct errors.
- Manage folders.
- Add new pages.
- Use the Site Trash.
- Manage and design your site using the Site view.
- Change hyperlinks and file references.
- Import resources, and remove unused resources.
- Restructure and export your site.
- Upload your site to a Web server.

This lesson will take you about an hour and a half to complete. If necessary, remove the previous lesson from your desktop and copy the Lesson08 folder onto it.

About Adobe GoLive Web site management

An Adobe GoLive Web site contains a site file, which it uses to manage and store data about the site. It is important that you do all your work, especially adding, removing, or renaming files, within the Adobe GoLive site file and not on the desktop. If you do add a file on the desktop, you will need to update your site window when you next open Adobe GoLive.

Another reason to work exclusively in Adobe GoLive is that it creates additional files and folders to contain the tools it uses to manage a site. For example, it creates a .data folder to hold components, stationeries, and Site Trash.

Getting started

In this lesson, you'll learn how to manage an existing Web site using Adobe GoLive.

1 Start Adobe GoLive.

2 Close Untitled.html.

3 Choose File > Open and open the Gage.site file.

The path is /Lesson08/08End/Gage.site.

This site contains a number of HTML pages and two folders, Animations and Images, that contain graphics files. When you have completed this lesson, your site will look like this.

4 If necessary, expand the site window:

• In Windows, click the arrow (▷) in the bottom left corner of the site window.

• In the Mac OS, click the icon (▨) on the top right corner of the site window.

The expanded pane of the site window contains three tabs: Errors, FTP, and Extra. If you open these tabs, you will find them empty. The organized site contains no errors or extras, and has not been uploaded to an FTP site.

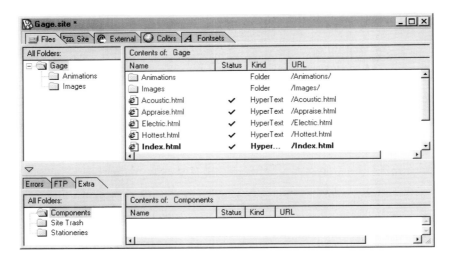

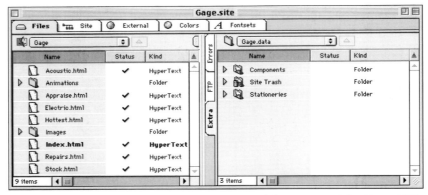

Gage site window, showing files and folder structure and the pane containing Errors, FTP, and Extra tabs

5 Close the Gage.site site window. This closes the Web site.

Importing an existing site into Adobe GoLive

You will now work with the files in the Start folder, which contains a non-Adobe GoLive site called Gage. Your first task is to import the site into Adobe GoLive.

1 Choose File > New Site > Import from Folder. Click the top Browse button and navigate to the 08Start folder. Select the Gage folder. This is the Web site you will import into Adobe GoLive format.

2 Click OK (Windows) or click Select "Gage" (Mac OS). The path to the folder is entered into the top text box of the Import Site Folder dialog box.

Because the site already has an Index.html page, Adobe GoLive recognizes this as the home page and automatically enters it into the bottom text box. If the Index.html page were missing, you would need to browse for the site's home page.

Note: *If a site folder is visible on your desktop, you can drag it straight to the top text box of the Import Site Folder dialog box.*

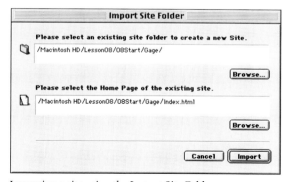

Importing a site using the Import Site Folder

3 Click Import.

The Web site is imported into the Adobe GoLive format, showing all its folders, files, and other site objects.

4 Choose File > Save As, name the file Gage.site and save it in the 08Start folder. (Be careful not to save it in the 08End folder.)

Exploring the site in the site window

In the site window, the Files tab shows all the objects in your site; you can use it to create, rename, move, and delete folders, files, and other site objects. The site has an Animations folder, some graphics files, and several HTML pages. Notice that some files have check marks in the Status column, indicating that their links are OK. Other files have little green bugs (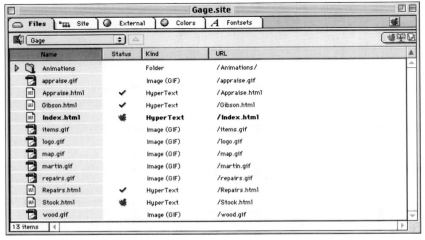) beside them, indicating that they contain broken links. These broken links show up in the Errors tab of the site window, which you will look at later in this lesson.

Displaying site in Files tab in site window

1 In the site window, select the Index.html file.

The Inspector changes to the File Inspector. This Inspector lets you rename files, manage their properties, see their contents, and change your home page. You can use it to manage a number of different file types, such as pages, images, and media files.

File Inspector

2 Click the Page tab of the File Inspector and notice that the Home Page option is selected, making this your home page. However, the option is inactive. The only way to designate another file as the home page is to open it and select its Home Page option.

3 In the site window, select Logo.gif. The File Inspector's tabs now reflect image properties.

4 Click the Content tab of the File Inspector to see a thumbnail of the image. Select another image, then a third.

You can use the Content tab of the Image Inspector to scroll through your images and search for the one you want.

5 Choose View > Link Inspector (Windows) or Window > Link Inspector (Mac OS). This opens the Link Inspector.

The Link Inspector shows links to the image from the HTML pages in which it appears. (Again, select several other images to see how the Link Inspector changes.) The Link Inspector is a very useful tool that enables you to see links, manage them, and correct them. Its point and shoot capability (⊚) lets you easily create and change links, or deal with broken links.

6 Click the Index.html page icon in the Link Inspector. The Inspector changes to show all links to and from that page. (If necessary, resize the Inspector window so that you can see all the links.)

If you click one of the links from Index.html, the focus of the Inspector changes again. In this way, you can use the Link Inspector to check all the links in your site. In addition, you can use the various Inspector windows to update and edit information about your site objects and their links.

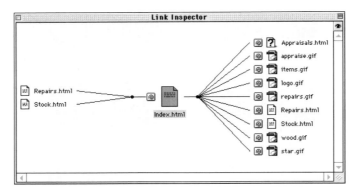

Link Inspector

7 Close the Link Inspector.

Exploring the expanded site window

You will now take a look at the features of the expanded site window.

1 Expand the site window:

• In Windows, click the arrow (▷) in the bottom left corner of the site window.

• In the Mac OS, click the icon (▣▣▣) in the top right corner of the site window.

You can drag the tab bar between the two panes to resize them, if you wish. You may also want to move the site window to the bottom of your screen. This will help you keep it in view when you open site files.

Note: *To collapse the expanded pane, click the icon at the top of the divider between the two panes.*

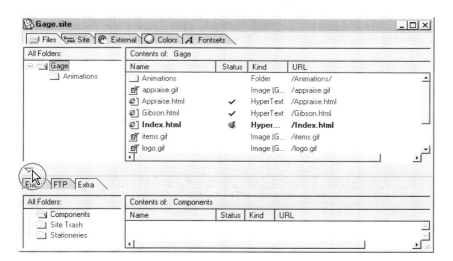

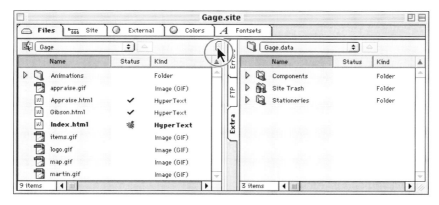

The expanded of the site window contains three tabs: Errors, FTP, and Extra.

2 Click the Extra tab to open it.

This tab contains three folders: Components, Site Trash, and Stationeries. These folders were created by Adobe GoLive and put into the Gage.data folder when you imported the site.

• Components are HTML pages that you can imbed inside others. You can make a single component and use it again and again. Examples include a navigation bar set up with its own images and links, a copyright pane, or formatted text.

• Site Trash contains any site objects you have removed from your site. From here, you can either drag them into the desktop Recycle Bin (Windows) or Trash (Mac OS), or drag them back to your site.

• Stationeries are page templates that may contain framesets, images, stylesheets, and so on, for repeated use.

At this point all three folders are empty.

3 Click the FTP tab to open it.

This tab is also empty. When connected to your FTP server, it lists all files and folders you have uploaded to the server, along with the date they were last revised.

4 Click the Errors tab to open it.

This tab lists any errors in your site. Notice that several types of errors appear in it: an orphan file, an unspecified link (or empty reference), and some missing hypertext links.

5 In Windows, click the Orphan Files folder to open it.

The one orphan file, Star.gif is displayed.

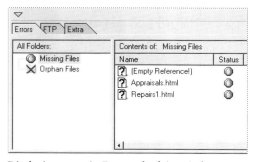

Displaying errors in Errors tab of site window

Correcting errors

You will now correct the errors displayed in the Errors tab. First, you'll solve the problem of the orphan file.

Resolving orphan files

An orphan file is one that is referenced in your site, but either can't be found, or is in the Site Trash. Use the Errors tab to check for problems, and be sure that you include the file before you upload your site onto a Web server. Copying the file into your site folder will fix the problem.

1 In the Errors tab, select the Star.gif file. Notice that the Inspector changes to the File Inspector. The Content tab displays the image, which is an animation that flashes on and off. This lets you confirm that you are working with the correct file.

2 Drag the file from the Errors tab to the Animations folder in the Files tab of the site window.

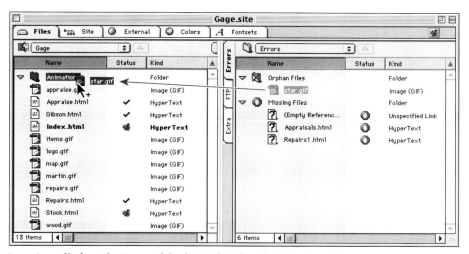

Dragging a file from the Errors tab back into the Files tab of the site window

3 Click OK in the Copy Files dialog box. This confirms that you want to copy the file into your site, and update its links.

If you are too slow dropping the file on the Animations folder, you may end up inside it. In Mac OS, you can return to the root folder by clicking the Navigation button (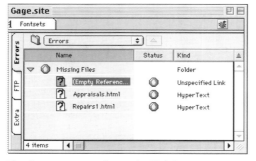) at the top of the Files tab.

Note: When you copy a file to your site window, your desktop also makes a copy. So a copy of Star.gif now exists both in the site window and inside the Gage folder on your desktop.

Correcting missing file and hypertext link errors

Now, you'll fix the missing file errors that appear on the Errors tab of the site window. Use the Link Inspector to find out which files contain the broken references or links. You can resolve missing file errors in at least three ways:

- By removing all references to the file.
- By changing all references to point to a new file.
- By browsing for the file from the Error Inspector and copying it to your site.

1 In the Errors tab of the site window, select the missing file that says (Empty reference!). Notice how the Inspector changes to the Error Inspector, and (Empty Reference!) appears in the URL text box.

2 Choose View > Link Inspector (Windows) or Window > Link Inspector (Mac OS). The Link Inspector shows the empty reference, and the file containing it, Stock.html.

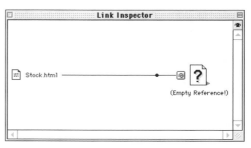

Viewing an empty reference in Link Inspector

3 Double-click on the Stock.html file in the Files tab of the site window. An image is missing from the top-left corner of the page. In its place is an empty image placeholder. If necessary, resize or move the Stock.html file so that you can clearly see the Files tab of the site window.

4 Select the image placeholder in Stock.html.

5 Press the Alt key (Windows) or the Command key (Mac OS), and drag a line from the image placeholder to the Logo.gif file on the Files tab of the site window. Release the mouse button. The black Gage logo appears on the page.

Adobe GoLive has removed the Empty Reference error warning from the site window.

Note: *If the Files tab is partially hidden, just hold the pointer over the part of it you can see, until the tab comes to the front.*

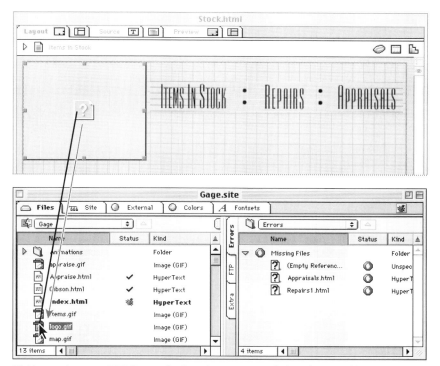

Linking an image to HTML page by dragging a Point and Shoot line to a file in the site window

There is also a broken hypertext link on this page, but this error is more difficult to find.

6 If necessary, resize or move the Stock.html file so you can see all its contents.

7 Click the Link Warnings button (![icon]) in the toolbar. The bad link is highlighted in red. (You may have to scroll down the page a little to see it.)

8 Double-click on the highlighted text (the word "Repairs") to select the link. The Inspector changes to the Text Inspector and the bad URL is highlighted in pink in its URL field.

9 In the Text Inspector, drag from the Point and Shoot button to the Repairs.html file in the Files tab. If the Files tab is partially hidden, hold your pointer over it until the tab comes to the front. If you can't see the Repairs.html file on the tab, you can scroll down the list of files if you hold your pointer down over the lowest visible file in the pane.

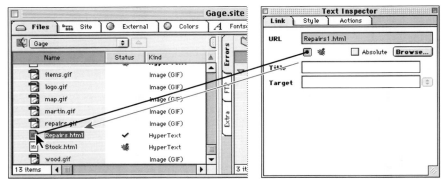

Using the Point and Shoot button on the Text Inspector to fix a broken link

The pink disappears from the URL field of the Text Inspector and from the word "Repairs". Notice that the Repairs1.html hypertext link warning has been removed. Click the Link Warnings button on the toolbar, and verify that there are no other broken links.

10 Choose File > Save to save your work. Close the Stock.html file.

Only one missing file error remains to be fixed. You will next use the Link Inspector to repair the connection to Appraisals.html.

11 Select Appraisals.html in the Errors tab of the site window. The Link Inspector shows that Index.html is the only page that contains a link to the missing file.

The link from Index.html refers to a file called Appraisals.html, but the Files tab contains one called Appraise.html. At some point, the file was renamed without updating all the links to it.

You will use the Point and Shoot feature in the Link Inspector to fix this error. Be sure that you can see both the site window and the Appraisals.html file in the Link Inspector.

12 Drag a line from the Point and Shoot button next to the Appraisals.html file to the Appraise.html file in the Files tab of the site window.

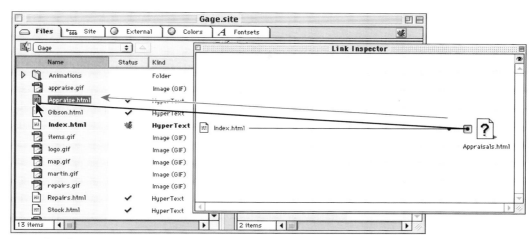

Fixing file references with Link Inspector

13 Click OK in the Change Reference dialog box to confirm that you want to change all references to the file.

14 Close the Link Inspector.

All the errors and bugs should now be gone and checkmarks should appear next to all your HTML pages in the Files tab, indicating that all their links are OK. In the Files tab, you can click the Kind column header to sort all your files by type. This will group all your HTML files and help you verify their links.

Note: *The Point and Shoot feature in the Link Inspector, Error Inspector, Text Inspector, the file itself, and the Errors Tab operates in the same way.*

Managing folders

You will now improve the organization of the Web site by rearranging its folders and files. Because Adobe GoLive dynamically updates all your links as you go, you don't have to worry about redoing them each time you change the files or folders.

Creating a folder and adding files to it

As your site grows, you will need to create folders to hold and organize all the files. You'll begin by creating a new folder for images, and move files into it.

1 Click anywhere in the Files tab of the site window to make it active. Be sure that you have the Gage (root) folder open.

2 Click the New Folder button on the Site toolbar (🗑).

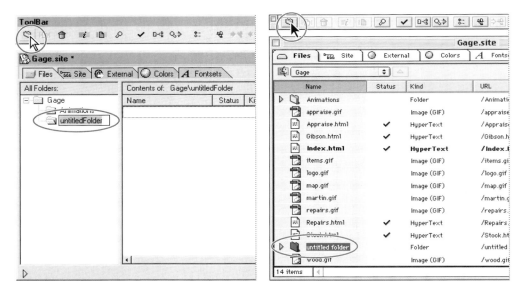

3 In Mac OS, click the title bar of the Inspector to change it to the Folder Inspector.

4 In the Name text box in the Folder Inspector, enter **Pix**. Then press Enter or Return, or click the Enter button (🔁). The name of the folder changes.

You can change the name of any folder or file either by selecting it in the Files tab and typing a new name directly over the old one, or by entering the new name in the Inspector.

5 In the Files tab, deselect the Pix folder. Control-click (Windows) or Shift-click (Mac OS) to select all the image files (any files with a .Gif extension) and the Animations folder.

In Windows, once you have selected all the items, release the Control key or you will copy rather than move them.

6 Drag the selected items into the Pix folder.

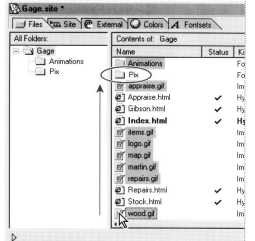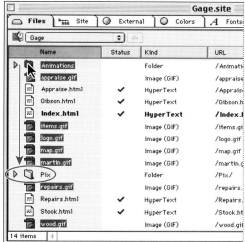

Dragging items into Pix folder

7 Click OK in the Move Files dialog box. Adobe GoLive dynamically updates all the links.

8 Choose File > Save to save the changes to your site.

Moving a folder

Next you'll move the Animations folder from the Pix folder back into the Gage folder, and update all its links.

1 Double-click the Pix folder in the site window, to open it if necessary.

2 Select the Animations folder and drag it to the Gage (root) folder:

• In Windows, drag the Animations folder from the right pane of the Files tab to the Gage folder in the left pane.

• In Mac OS, drag the Animations folder to the Navigation button ( ) at the top of the Files tab, but don't release the mouse button. If you do, the folder will return to the Pix folder. When the root folder springs open, drag the Animations folder to the Name bar at the top of the Files tab, and then release the mouse button.

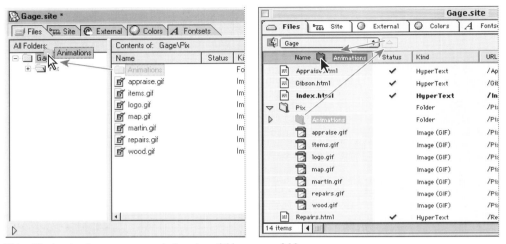

Using Navigation button to move Animations folder to root folder

3 Click OK in the Move Files dialog box. The Animations folder appears in the root folder, and all the links are updated.

Renaming a folder

Now, you'll rename the Pix folder to Images. But first, you'll open the Explorer file management application(Windows), so that you can see how changes made inside Adobe GoLive automatically update your desktop. In Mac OS the Finder automatically displays all the changes on your desktop.

1 Resize the Adobe GoLive application window to half of your screen size. Keep the site window in view.

2 Open the Pix folder through your operating system:

• In Windows, select the Pix folder and click the Reveal Item button ( ) on the toolbar. You can also right click the Pix folder and choose Reveal in Explorer. Resize the Explorer window and drag it next to the Adobe GoLive application window.

• In Mac OS, select the Pix folder and click the Reveal in Finder button (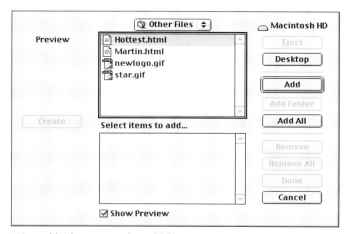) on the toolbar. You can also Command-click the Pix folder in the Files tab. If necessary, resize the window and drag it next to the site window.

You should have both the Adobe GoLive and Explorer (Windows) or Finder (Mac OS) windows visible side-by-side.

3 In the Files tab in the site window, change the name of the Pix folder to **Images**. Press Enter or Return.

4 Click OK in the Rename Folder dialog box to confirm that you want to update the files.

Notice how the folder name has also changed on your desktop. Adobe GoLive works with your operating system to ensure reliability of the links within your site.

5 Close the Explorer (Windows) or other windows on your desktop.

Adding new pages to your site

You are now going to add two new pages to your site using two different techniques. Each method automatically copies the file and places it in your site folder, without moving the original file.

You'll first add a file using the Add Files command.

1 In the site window, select the Gage folder.

2 Choose Site > Add Files and navigate to the Other Files folder inside your 08Start folder. Open it and select the Hottest.html file.

Using Add Files command to add file to your site

3 Click Add; then click Done. You should see Hottest.html in the Files tab in the site window.

Now, you'll add another file by dragging it from the Explorer (Windows) or the desktop (Mac OS) to your site.

4 In the Explorer (Windows) or the desktop (Mac OS), navigate to the Other Files folder inside your 08Start folder. If necessary, resize the windows.

5 Drag the Martin.html file from the Other Files folder to the Gage folder in the Files tab in the site window.

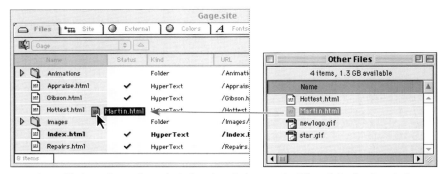

Dragging a file from the Explorer (Windows) or desktop to the Files tab in the site window

Notice how the two newly added files appear in the Gage folder window that is open in the Explorer (Windows) or on the desktop (Mac OS).

6 Close the Explorer (Windows) or any desktop windows (Mac OS).

Note: *If you remove or add files from within folders in the Explorer (Windows) or on the desktop (Mac OS) without copying them into Adobe GoLive, you must use the Update button (✔) on the Site toolbar to include or remove the files in your site.*

Using the Site Trash

You use the Site Trash to remove, but not permanently discard, a site object that you no longer want to be included in your site. By using the Site Trash you can later retrieve it, including all its links. Move a site object to the Site Trash by dragging it to the Site Trash tab, or selecting the object and clicking the Delete Selected Item button (🗑) on the Site toolbar.

Now you'll remove a file from your site that you no longer need, but think you may want to keep.

1 In the Files tab of the site window, select the Gibson.html file.

2 Click the Delete Selected Item button (🗑) in the Site toolbar.

3 Click OK. This moves the file to the Site Trash.

If you want to retrieve an object, drag it from the Site Trash folder in the site window to the Files tab, and update its links.

1 Open the Extra tab in the expanded site window.

2 Double-click the Site Trash folder and find Gibson.html.

3 Drag Gibson.html from the Site Trash folder to the Files tab of the site window.

4 Click OK to update the links.

To permanently remove an object from your site:

• Select it and press the Delete key.

• Drag it into the Recycle Bin (Windows) or Trash (Mac OS).

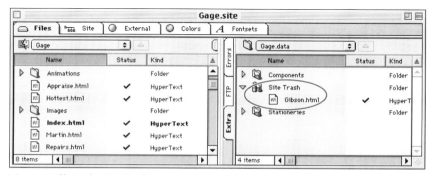

Viewing a file in the Site Trash

Changing Site Trash Preferences

You can change what Adobe GoLive does when you move items to the Site Trash by changing preferences. By default items are not permanently thrown away, and you are warned before they are moved. To permanently discard site items:

1. Choose Edit > Preferences to open the Preferences dialog box.

2. Select Site, then choose Move them to the system trash (Windows) or Move them to the Finder Trash (Mac OS).

This option sends all selected items straight to the system Recycle Bin or Trash, and not the Site Trash.

3. Click OK.

Managing the Site view

The Site view is a powerful tool for controlling your site. You can view your site in Link Hierarchy, Navigation Hierarchy, and Outline views. It gives you simple diagrams of your site, and lets you manage links and pages. Here, you will use it to check the links in your site, add pages, and create links to them.

1 Click the Site tab of the site window to open the Site view.

2 If necessary, click the eye icon ( ) at the top of the vertical scrollbar, or choose View > Inspector (Windows) or Window > Inspector (Mac OS) to open the Site View Controller.

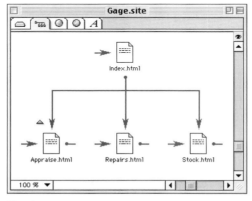

Site view

Site View Controller

The Site view shows the Index.html page at the top of the site hierarchy and three other pages on the level below. There are link indicators into (➡) and out of (•—) pages, which show links to and from pages that are located in other parts of the site hierarchy.

3 Click on one of the Appraise.html link indicators. This opens the Link Inspector and shows all the links to and from that page.

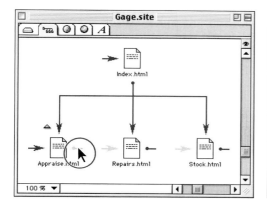 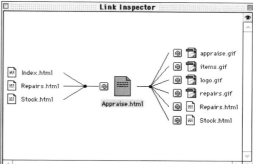

Selecting link indicator to view its links in Link Inspector

4 Select another link indicator. The Link Inspector changes to display that page.

5 Close the Link Inspector when you have finished.

You can also collapse and expand parts of your site hierarchy. This is especially useful if you have a large site.

6 Move the pointer over the Index.html page icon until a down arrow appears below it. Click the arrow. The site collapses into the Index.html page icon.

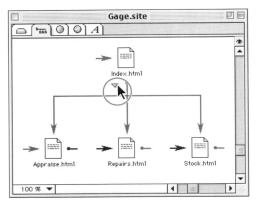

Collapsing site hierarchy into Index.html page icon　　　　*Result*

7 Move the pointer over the Index.html multi-page icon until a right-pointing arrow appears below it. Click the arrow. The site expands to show all the other pages.

These are a few of the features the Link Hierarchy offers. You can also use the Navigation Hierarchy.

8 Click anywhere in the Site view window to deselect the Index.html page.

9 On the Arrange tab of the Site View Controller, select Navigation Hierarchy. (You can also choose this mode from the Navigation Hierarchy button ( ) on the Site toolbar.) Use this mode to arrange and navigate across the objects in your site.

The Site View Controller has four tabs that let you to set the Site view's Arrange, Filter, Display, and Color properties. Take a look at the tabs and their options.

10 Click the Filter tab of the Site View Controller. This tab lets you choose which site objects you want to see in the Site view. Select HTML Files and Media Files. Notice how the content of the Site view has changed. All the media files in your site are shown alongside the HTML pages.

11 Drag the horizontal scrollbar on the Site view to the right to see all the added media files.

12 Select the If Unreachable option.

13 The two pages you recently added to your site, Martin.html and Hottest.html, as well as an unreachable image file, Martin.gif are displayed. If necessary, scroll to see the files.

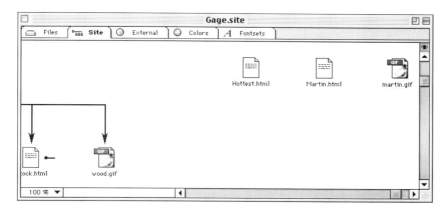

Adobe GoLive also provides an Outline view of the site hierarchy.

14 Click the Display tab of the Site View Controller and, at the bottom of the Display tab, select Outline.

The Outline mode displays a tabular view of your site. In Mac OS, it also provides information about each object's status, type (Kind), and URL.

15 In the Outline mode, click on the icon next to the Index.html page to expand the tree view. In this mode, you can expand and contract the view, as well as move site objects.

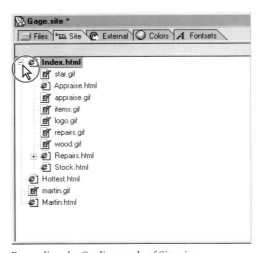
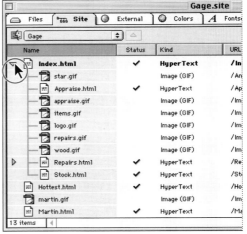

Expanding the Outline mode of Site view

16 In the Display tab of the Site View Controller, select Site View to return to a hierarchical view of your site.

17 If necessary, click the blank space in the Site view to open the Site View Controller.

18 In the Display tab, try out some of the other view options. When you have finished, select Icons, File Name, and Site View; set the Horizontal grid value to **55** and the Vertical grid value to **140**.

Using the Site Navigator

Your monitor may not be large enough to display your entire site, so Adobe GoLive has a Site Navigator to help you move throughout the entire hierarchical view. The Site Navigator is a separate window that displays your whole site and has a marquee that highlights the part of your site currently visible in the Site view.

1 Click the Open Site Navigator button (▦) (Windows) or (▦) (Mac OS) in the Site toolbar.

2 Place the pointer within the marquee in the Site Navigator, and use the hand to drag the marquee back and forth across the site. Notice how the Site view changes as you move the marquee.

3 Close the Site Navigator window when you have finished viewing your site.

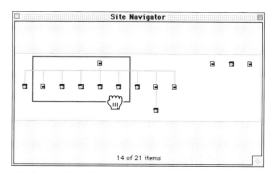

Moving the Site Navigator marquee

Inserting pages into your site hierarchy

As you can see, the two new pages you added to your site, Hottest.html and Martin.html, aren't part of the main hierarchy yet. This is because you haven't created links to them, so they are unreachable from the rest of your site. One of these pages is ready for public viewing, so you'll link it to the rest of your site.

1 Click the Filter tab on the Site View Controller and deselect Media Files. This will make it easier to manage your pages. If necessary, scroll or resize the hierarchy window and find the unreachable files.

2 Click the Navigation Hierarchy button on the site toolbar.

3 Drag the Hottest.html page below the Index.html page, and drop it when the blue down arrow appears. The Hottest.html page moves under the Index.html page, to the right of the Stock.html page. Notice the dotted line to the Index.html page, which indicates that there is still no link between these pages.

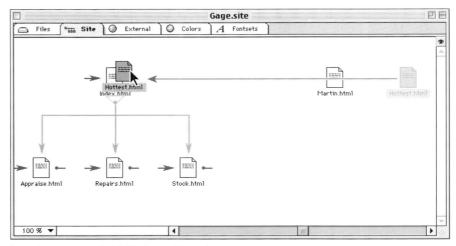

Inserting an unreachable file in site hierarchy

When you drag pages over other pages in the hierarchy, blue arrows can appear above, below, or on the same hierarchical level as an existing file, allowing you to drop pages wherever you want in the tree.

4 Leave the Martin.html file where it is. It is still under construction.

Creating links between pages using the Site view

Now you'll create the link from the Index.html page to the Hottest.html page.

1 In the Site view, double-click the Index.html page to open it.

2 If necessary, resize or move the Index.html page so that you can see both the Site view and the "Check Out This Week's Hottest Buy" text.

3 Select the text "Check Out This Week's Hottest Buy."

4 Hold down Alt (Windows) or Command (Mac OS) and drag a Point and Shoot line from the selected text to the Hottest.html page in the Site view. (This page may be partially hidden by the Index.html page, but hold the pointer over the window until the Site view is brought to the front.)

The Text Inspector shows the new link to the Hottest.html page in the URL field. In the Site view notice that the line to the Hottest.html page is now solid, indicating a solid link.

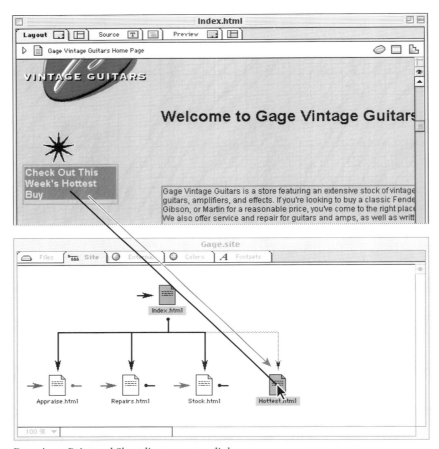

Dragging a Point and Shoot line to create a link

5 Save and close the Index.html page.

Creating new pages in the Site view

Your site needs two new pages featuring your latest items. You can do this directly from the Site view window.

1 In the Site view, move your pointer over the Stock.html page icon. The Create New Page live button($\square$) (Windows) or ($\boxed{\square}$) (Mac OS) appears above, below, or to the side of the page. This button lets you add new pages above, below, or on the same hierarchical level as an existing page.

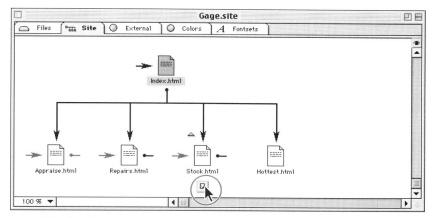

Create New Page live button

2 Click the Create New Page live button when it appears beneath the Stock.html page. A new, untitled page appears below the Stock.html page. If necessary, use the Site Navigator marquee or the vertical scrollbar to see this new page.

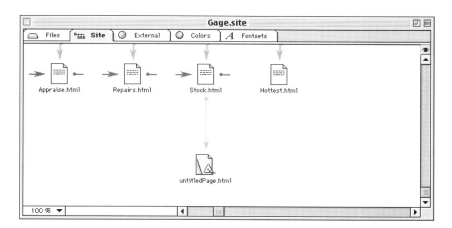

3 Repeat Step 2 to create another untitled page. Notice that both new pages appear on the same level of the hierarchy.

Note: *If you make a mistake and add a page where you don't want it, select the page and click the Delete Selected Item button (🗑) in the Site toolbar. Then confirm that you want to move the page to the Site Trash.*

4 Select the names of the new pages and change them to Acoustic.html and Electric.html.

Dotted green lines appear between these new pages and their parent page, indicating that there are no links to these pages yet. You'll finish the links in the next section.

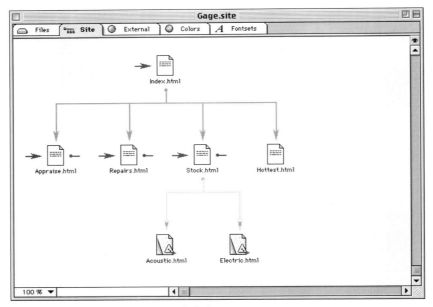

Dotted green lines indicating missing links between pages

Creating links to new pages using the Site view

Now you'll link these two new pages to the rest of your site using the Site view. First, you'll link Acoustic.html to Stock.html.

1 In the Site view, double-click the Stock.html page icon to open the page.

2 Select "Acoustic Guitars" at the bottom of the page.

3 Hold down Alt (Windows) or Command (Mac OS) and drag a Point and Shoot line from the selected text to the Acoustic.html page icon in the Site view. This links the text to the page.

4 Select "Electric Guitars" at the bottom of the page

5 Repeat Step 3, this time linking the text to the Electric.html page icon in the Site view.

6 Save and close the Stock.html page.

7 Refresh the screen by selecting another icon.

The links to the Acoustic.html and Electric.html pages are now solid lines. You have just created two new pages, remapped your site hierarchy, and linked them to other pages.

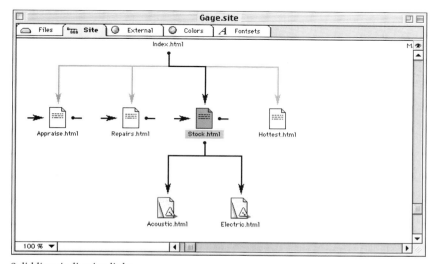

Solid lines indicating links

Moving newly created files into the root folder

Whenever you create new pages in the Site view, Adobe GoLive creates a NewFiles (Windows) or New Pages (Mac OS) folder in the Files tab of the site window to hold them. This is a useful place to keep files that are under construction, but now you'll move the files into another folder.

1 Click the Files tab in the site window to open it. Then open the NewFiles or New Pages folder to display the new Acoustic.html and Electric.html pages.

There are two yellow icons (⚠) next to these pages, which indicate that they are under construction. The icons will disappear once you start adding content.

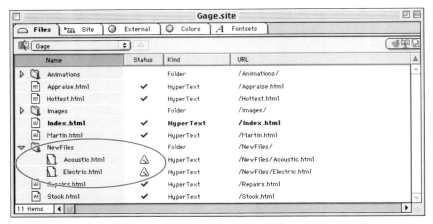

Under Construction icons appearing next to the two new files

2 Shift-click to select the two pages and drag them to the Gage (root) folder, and update the links.

In Mac OS, remember that you have to drag files up to the Name bar at the top of the Files tab to drop them into the root folder.

Changing all hyperlinks and file references

When you remove a page and replace it with another, at the same time you can dynamically transfer all the links to the page. This also applies to changing an image that occurs throughout your site. The Change References option is a simple way to do this.

You'll try this feature by changing the logo image that appears on most pages of the Gage site from Logo.gif to Newlogo.gif.

1 Double-click the Index.html file in the Files tab of the site window. You'll find the Gage Vintage Guitars logo in the top-left corner of the page. This is the image you are going to change.

2 If necessary, resize the Index.html so that you can clearly see both the site window and the logo.

3 Select the Logo.gif file in the Images folder in the Files tab of the site window.

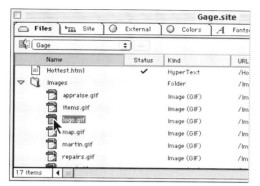 

4 Choose Site > Change References. Browse to the Other Files folder in the 08Start folder and open Newlogo.gif. The new file path appears in the Change References dialog box.

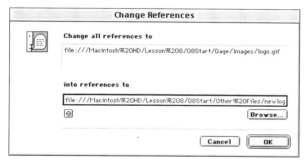

Browsing for Newlogo.gif file

5 Click OK, then confirm that you want to change all references to the image.

All references to the old file are changed, and the new logo appears in the Index.html page.

New logo displayed in Index.html page

6 Save and close the Index.html page.

If you want to check that the logos on other pages have been updated, open those pages.

Importing resources and removing unused ones

Your site now has a file that you don't want (Logo.gif), and a file referenced by your site that is not in the site folder (Newlogo.gif). The latter is an orphan file; it appears in the Errors tab in the site window. You'll import the Newlogo.gif file into your site using the Clear Site dialog box. At the same time, you'll remove Logo.gif and any other unused files and non-file objects, such as URLs and e-mail addresses.

1 Choose Site > Clear Site. Select all the Add used and Remove unused options. Click OK.

Note: *Clearing the site rescans the whole site and updates it; it also updates the files on your desktop.*

The Clear Site dialog box shows that the Newlogo.gif file is referenced in the site, but is not included in the site folder.

2 Click OK to copy the Newlogo.gif file into the site folder.

A list of all the files that need to be updated appears in the Copy Files dialog box.

3 Click OK to update them.

A list appears of unreferenced files that will be sent to the Site Trash. They are Logo.gif, Martin.gif, and Martin.html.

4 Click OK to remove these objects from your site.

Note: *You can prevent any file from going to the Trash by deselecting the option next to it. However, it will remain unlinked and unused.*

In the Errors tab of the site window, notice that the orphan file error has been resolved. Adobe GoLive has moved the orphan file (Newlogo.gif) into the NewFiles folder in the Files tab of the site window.

5 Select Newlogo.gif and move it into the Images folder, and update the links to it.

6 Trash the empty NewFiles folder by selecting it and clicking the Delete selected item button.

7 Save your site.

Congratulations! You have completed the Adobe GoLive 4.0 Classroom in a Book. You have learned the essential concepts and skills necessary to master the application. You created Web pages with graphics, worked with text, animation, CGI forms, cascading stylesheets, and prepared your site for presentation.

The last step is to upload your site to a Web server, so the world can enjoy your work. Because this requires certain hardware and software not included with the Adobe GoLive 4.0 package, you can try this on your own.

Exploring on your own

Before Internet viewers can visit your site, you must copy it to an FTP site on a server. Your Internet service provider can help you with the details of uploading and maintaining your site.

Uploading your site to a Web server

Once you create your own site, you will want to upload it to an FTP site on a Web server, where it can be viewed by people visiting your site. Adobe GoLive has two FTP tools:

• A built-in FTP tool that is an integral part of the site window. Use this to upload your site to the Web server or to edit pages remotely.

• A standalone FTP Upload & Download window. Use this to access FTP servers on the Web and upload or download files from within the application.

You will upload your site using the second of these methods. For further details about the built-in FTP tool, see the *Adobe GoLive 4.0 User Guide*.

1 Make sure that you have properly set up the PPP, TCP/IP, and modem settings on your computer. Also, be sure that you have the following:

• Access rights to a Web server.

• The server's name and the directory you want.

• Your user ID and password.

2 Choose File > FTP Upload/Download. This opens the FTP Upload & Download dialog box.

3 Type the FTP address of the Web server you want to access in the Server text box.

4 In the Directory text box, type in the directory path to the folder on the FTP site or Web server where you want your site to be placed.

Note: In most cases, you will only have access to one folder, so you won't need to enter anything in this text box.

5 In the User Name text box, type in your user ID. Then click the pop-up menu next to this text box and add the server to your preferences.

6 Type your password in the Password text box if necessary.

7 Click Connect. This connects you to the server. Once you are logged on, the contents of the directory you chose on the server are displayed in the All Files pane of the dialog box.

8 To upload your site, select all the files and folders in your site and drag them into the All Files pane of the FTP Upload & Download dialog box.

9 Once the files and folders have been uploaded, close the dialog box.

The files and folders on the FTP site or Web server appear in the FTP tab of the site window when you click the FTP Server Connect/Disconnect button on the site toolbar. The date they were uploaded will also appear. You can update files on the FTP site or Web server at any time by opening the FTP Upload & Download dialog box and dragging the new files to the FTP directory.

Review questions

1 What is an orphan file and how do you fix it?

2 How do you create a new folder and move files into it? What happens once you move the files?

3 How do you recover a file you have removed and sent to the Site Trash?

4 What are the two ways to add a file to your site from a folder outside your site?

5 How do you create a new page icon in the Site view below an existing page icon?

6 How do you create a link from some text in a parent page to a child page using the Site view?

Review answers

1 An orphan file is one that is referenced in your site, but either isn't in the folder to which it is referenced, or has been removed to the Site Trash. You fix it either by moving it back into the folder to which it is referenced, by changing references to it, or by dragging the file from the Site Trash back to your site.

2 You use the New Folder button to create a new folder. You can add files to it either by dragging them to the folder (if they are already in your site) or by using the Add Files command (if they are not in your site). Once you move files that are already in your site into the new folder, Adobe GoLive dynamically updates the links to these files.

3 You can recover a file from the Site Trash by dragging it back to the Files tab in the site window.

4 You can add a file to your site from outside either by using the Add Files command or by dragging from the outside folder to the Files tab in the site window.

5 You pass the pointer over the existing page icon until the Create New Page live button appears below it. Click the live button and rename the new page icon.

6 Open the parent page, select the text, click the New Link button on the Site toolbar, then create the link by:

• Dragging a Point and Shoot line directly from the text to the child page icon in the Site view.

• Using the Point and Shoot button in the Text Inspector.

• Using the Point and Shoot button in the Link Inspector.

Index

A

absolute paths 135

actions
   adding 138, 201
   adding to animations 204–207
   adding to rollover 203
   defined 200
   link 181
   mouse 139
   On Load 202
   rollover 179
   sizing windows 139

aligning and distributing objects 91

anchors
   creating 129–132
   placing 129
   text 129
   verifying 131

animation
   adding actions 204–207
   floating boxes 189
   keyframes 189
   path, editing 193–194
   several floating boxes 195–200

B

Bold button 52

Border Size option 163

broken links 149

button image
   Click 181
   Main 180
   Over 181

buttons
   "eye" 296
   Add Row 63
   Align Top 91
   Bold 52

Create New Page 305

Decrease List Level 54

Delete Selected Item 295

Equidistant Edges 91

Increase List Level button 54

Italic 52

Left Align 62

Link Warnings 287

Loop 192

Navigation Hierarchy 298

New Folder 290

New Link 126

New Tag 255

Numbered List 53

Palindrome 192

Play 191

Plus 264

Preview Frame 169

Remove Link 133

Select Color 144

Show in Browser 131

Site Navigator 301

Stop 192

TimeLine Editor 189

Trash 306

Unnumbered List 53

Vertical Align Center 111

C

Cascading Style Sheets. *See* CSS. 243

Cell Pad option 58

Change References option 308

changing file references 308

Clear Site 310

Color Palette 49

color palette
   custom 98
   updating custom 103

Common Gateway Interface (CGI)
   defined 213

Create New Page button 305

CSS
   .css extension 259
   adding a new style 254–256
   background color 265
   Cascading defined 261
   changing and comparing style
      sheets 269
   class selectors defined 262
   creating 257–258
   creating a class selector 262–263
   defined 243
   duplicating a style 264
   editing 253
   external style sheet defined 257
   internal style sheet defined 257
   internal style sheet, exploring 246
   linking to documents 259
   previewing 267
   saving 259
   style sheet selectors 249–250
   turning on and off 247
   updating 251–253
   weight 261

D

Document Layout Controller 69

dynamic components
   defined 83
   editing 110

E

editing text 67–68

Empty Reference Warning 87

End Form tags 214

F

file references, changing 308

files, absolute paths 135

find and replace 67–68

floating boxes

    adding 106

    adding images 106–109, 186

    animating 189

    animating several 195–200

    creating 184–185

    defined 182

    keyframes 189

    locking 196–197

    naming 185

    stacking order 188, 199

    using 104

Font Set Editor 65

fonts, applying 65–67

form tags

    End Form 214

    Form 214

forms

    adding address fields 219

    adding an image 227

    adding clickable images 232

    adding fields 217–220

    adding list box 231

    adding name fields 217

    adding pop-up menus 222

    adding radio buttons 228

    adding Reset button 234

    adding Submit button 234

    adjusting columns 226

    border and cell 224

    borders 235

    creating with tables 216–217

    custom elements 224–226

    defined 214

    inserting tables 216

    tab order 235

Frame Editor tab 161

frame sets

    adding 161–162

adding frames 167

adding scroll bars 167

changing 163

contents frame 165

creating 161

defined 158

deleting frames 167

    Scale 166

    Size menu 166

    Vertical Orientation option 164

frames, adding content 169–170

FTP Upload and Download 313

H

home pages

    adding page components 94

    background images 93

    designing 93

HTML

    declaration 243

    rule 243

    selector 243

HTML Outline Editor 71

HTML Source Editor 70

hyperlinks

    changing 308

    repairing 287

hypertext links, creating 132–133

I

image maps

    creating 140–144

    hot spot colors 144

    hot spots 142

    inserting images 141

    linking 146

    testing 148

images

    adding 86–90

    image maps 140

    previewing in File Inspector 93

Increase List Level 54

Inspectors

    Action 202

    Button 180

    Component 95

    CSS Selector 245

    External Style Sheet 269

    File 93, 281

    Floating Box 106, 184

    Folder 290

    Form Button 234

    Form Image 233

    Form List Box 231

    Form Radio Button 229

    Form Text Field 236

    Frame 165

    Frame Set 163

    Image 126

    Keyframe 199

    Layout Grid 101

    Link 282

    Multiselection 91

    Page 49, 84

    Site 296

    Table 57, 216

Italic button 52

K

keyframes

    controlling floating boxes 190

    creating 189

    editing 192

    moving 191

L

layout text boxes 95

Left Align 62

line breaks in text 54

links

    about 120

    broken 149

    color 136–137

    correcting missing files with Link
        Inspector 286

creating by browsing 133
creating with URL 133
dynamic components 124
highlight 136–137
hypertext 132
image maps 140, 146
targeted 171
to homepage 172
to new frame set 173
troubleshooting 149
using graphics 123–128
using Point and Shoot 126
warning preferences 149
Loop button 192

M
menus
Action 203
Col. (Column) Separator 61
Execute 202
Floating Box 203
Font Size 62
FPS (Frames Per Second) 192
Frame Border 149
Horizontal Alignment 220
Mode 204
Paragraph Format 51
Root 249
Vertical Alignment 220
Window Size 49
mouse rollovers 179

N
Numbered List button 53

O
objects, aligning and distributing 91
orphaned file 285

P
page title 48
pages
adding images 86–90

adding text 50
changing background color 49–50
designing 48
dynamic components, creating 83
floating boxes 104
layout grid 85
previewing 69, 111
updating design 101
Palindrome button 192
paths, absolute 135
Play button 191
Preferences 67
preferences, URL handling 135
previewing Web pages 69

R
rollover actions 203

S
Site 302
Site Navigator
defined 301
including new pages 302
Site view
adding icons 305
including new pages 302
Link Hierarchy 298
linking new pages 306
linking pages 303
moving new files 307
Navigation Hierarchy 298
Site View Control-ler 296
site window
Components folder 284
dragging and dropping contents 81
Errors tab 284
exploring 283–284
Extra tab 284
FTP tab 284
Site Trash 284
Stationaries folder 284
sites
adding files 81–82

adding folders 81
adding new pages 293
creating 79
creating folders 290
error handling 285
home page 279
importing 279
managing folders 290
missing file error, correcting 286–289
moving folders 291
orphaned file 285
renaming folders 292
site folder contents 80
site link indicators 297
Site Trash 295
Site view 296
Trash, retrieving items 295
Trash, viewing contents 295
updating with Clear Site 310
uploading to server 312–313
Source tab 162
Stop button 192
Style Sheet toolbar 245
style sheet window 249

T
tables
adding captions 62
adding data 59–61
adding rows 63
changing cell color 64
formatting 61–65
formatting column headings 63
importing text 60
targeted links 171
text
adding 50
adding tables 56–59
changing color 55, 98
copy and paste 50
drag and drop 50
editing 67–68

floating boxes 50

formatting 51

layout text boxes 50, 95

line breaks 54

lists 52–54

styles 51

using with tables 97

text anchors 129

TimeLine Editor, multiple tracks 196

transitions

adding 205

Wipe 206

Wipe In From Top To Bottom 207

Trash button 306

U

Unnumbered List 53

URL Handling Preferences, absolute
paths 135

W

Web pages. *See* pages. 48

Web sites. *See* sites 279

Web sites. *See* sites. 79

window size, setting default 49

Also from Adobe Press

For more information on Adobe Press books, visit www.adobe.com.

Classroom in a Book

Classroom in a Book, the world's best-selling series of hands-on software training workbooks, offers complete self-paced training based on real-world projects. Books include intermediate and advanced techniques for both Windows and Macintosh. Use the specially created files on the CD-ROM as you work through the lessons and special projects in the book.

Print Publishing Guide and Electronic Publishing Guide

An essential resource for publishing professionals and novices, these books provide succinct, expertly illustrated explanations of the basic concepts and issues involved in electronic and print production, along with Adobe's tried and true guidelines, tips, and checklists for ensuring high-quality output.

Adobe Photoshop 5.0 Productivity Kit

Twenty-six ready-made projects developed by the creative staff of Adobe to help you get the most out of your photographs. CD-ROM includes 125 Photoshop, ImageReady, and PageMaker templates, backgrounds and actions. Step-by-step instructions and design and production tips ensure quick, professional results.

Design Essentials, Third Edition

This is the completely revised third edition of the bestselling *Design Essentials*. This creative guide provides innovative and inspiring design techniques broken down into illustrated steps.

Web Sites That Work

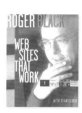

By celebrated designer Roger Black, with Sean Elder, Web reviewer for the New Yorker, this book brings Black's extensive experience in design to the competitive arena of the Web. Aimed at site creators, graphic designers, corporate managers, and advertising agencies, this book combines a sophisticated aesthetic with a practical approach to understanding the Web.

Adobe Certified Expert Program

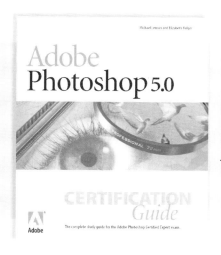

The Adobe Photoshop 5.0 Certification Guide contains comprehensive study material as well as Practice Proficiency Exams to help better prepare users for the Adobe Photoshop Proficiency Examination!

What is an ACE?

An Adobe Certified Expert is an individual who has passed an Adobe Product Proficiency Exam for a specific Adobe software product. Adobe Certified Experts are eligible to promote themselves to clients or employers as highly skilled, expert-level users of Adobe software. ACE certification is a recognized worldwide standard for excellence in Adobe software knowledge.

An Adobe Certified Training Provider (ACTP) is a certified teacher or trainer who has passed an Adobe Product Proficiency Exam. Training organizations that use ACTPs can become certified as well. Adobe promotes ACTPs to customers who need training.

ACE Benefits

When you become an ACE, you enjoy these special benefits:
- Professional recognition
- An ACE program certificate
- Use of the Adobe Certified Expert program logo

Additional benefits for ACTPs:

- Listing on the Adobe Web site
- Access to beta software releases when available
- *Classroom in a Book* in PDF

For information on the ACE and ACTP programs, go to partners.adobe.com, and look for Certified Training Programs under the Support section.